THE
FOLKLORE
OF
WARWICKSHIRE

Also published by LLanerch:

The Folklore of Plants
T F Thiselton Dyer

The Sacred Tree
J. H. Philpot

County Folklore: Northumberland
M C Balfour

Drolls, Traditions & Superstitions of Old Cornwall
Robert Hunt

The Gododdin
Steve Short

Taliesin Poems
Meirion Pennar

Celtic Folktales from Armorica
F M Luzel

The Celtic Legend of the Beyond
Anatole LeBraz.

For a complete list of small-press editions and facsimile reprints, 100+ titles, write to Llanerch Publishers, Felinfach, Lampeter, Dyfed, Wales. SA48 8PJ.

The Folklore
of Warwickshire

ROY PALMER
Drawings by Gay John Galsworthy

A facsimile reprint, 1994,
Llanerch Publishers
Felinfach.

First published by
B T Batsford Ltd, 1976.
Copyright © Roy Palmer, 1976
Facsimile reprint 1994
Llanerch Publishers

ISBN 1 897853 46 7

Contents

Acknowledgments

The Author and Publishers wish to acknowledge permission to quote from the following (page references are to *The Folklore of Warwickshire*): M. Ashby, *Joseph Ashby of Tysoe*, Cambridge University Press, 1961 (pp. 49, 165); J. H. Bird, *Sam Bennett*, Stratford-on-Avon, 1952 (p. 31, verses 1, 3, 4); J. Byng, *The Torrington Diaries*, Eyre and Spottiswoode, 1934-8 (p. 16); J. H. Bloom, *Folklore, Old customs and superstitions in Shakespeare land*, Mitchell, Hughes and Clarke, 1930 (pp. 31-2, verses 2, 5-8); *Folklore* Vol. 71, 1960 (pp. 112-3): M. Karpeles, *Cecil Sharp's Collection of English Folk Songs*, Oxford University Press, 1974 (p. 147); J. Lancaster, *Godiva of Coventry*, Corporation of Coventry, 1967 (p. 135); G. S. Miles, 'They're changing dear old Brummagem', (pp. 152-3); R. Palmer, *Songs of the Midlands*, E. P. Publishing, 1972 (p. 148)

Foreword

Samuel Timmins, writing nearly 90 years ago, imagined a series of lines drawn between different peripheral points around England, and all crossing in Warwickshire. Historically, too, the county is in some respects England's heartland. The name Martimow, in Radway parish, still commemorates the old frontier between the Hwiccan Saxons and the Mercian kingdom. This long survived as the boundary between Worcester and Lichfield Dioceses, bisecting the county. It is convincingly argued in Warwickshire *Place-Names* that the political frontier was sufficiently recollected in the mid-13th century to survive in contemporary terminology.

The pre-1974 county, covered by this book, existed for over a thousand years, and internal boundaries are one of its notable features. Place names provide clear evidence that this was recognised locally, and, apart from the Anglo-Saxon dividing line, Watling Street, still county border in the north-east, became the western limit of the Danelaw.

Dugdale, quoting common local terms for the afforested and open ('field') regions, noted in 1656 a clear division between the *Wood-land*, north of the Avon, and the *Feldon*, to the south. Rolt, a later traveller, crossing the Midlands by narrow boat some 35 years ago, entered the Oxford Canal at Hawkesbury near Coventry, relieved to pass an imaginary border, and head 'for open country once more, after so many miles on the sooty fringes of the Black Country'. Much of the Shire's industrial north has gone into the new West Midlands County, but Rolt's route south from Fazeley lay mostly through parishes still administered from Warwick today.

He described the county's northern mining area, and noted that 'such farm buildings as remained stood empty and were fast falling into ruin. What we could not see, but could picture most vividly, was the inhuman darkness of the narrow galleries below, the heat, the choking dust and the din of the coal-cutting machines, the hell below earth that the demand for power has created.' That night he

7

moored near Pooley Hall, an old mansion standing beside a colliery, where 'this new world met the old'.

But the underlying contrast is false. Just as the Mercian-Hwiccan frontier retained a notional existence four centuries after Mercia's collapse, so Warwickshire's unity has survived division into industrial and agricultural areas. Even the new West Midlands, rationalising this situation, is unlikely to wipe out the old identity very rapidly. 'Ride a cock-horse to Coventry Cross' – more unfamiliar than the Banbury version – long ago revealed, at least in children's rhymes, a common taste overriding differences between the industrial and rural Midlands. And more recently, the triumphs of Aston Villa have been as welcome in Warwickshire as among their supporters in Birmingham. Folk culture, almost unconsciously, is often aware of its roots.

Charlie Williams jokes: 'I went over to Birmingham. What a lovely country that is . . .' Successful comedians base their material on real life, so echoes of the same outlook from a different source, and in another context, are no surprise. Sir Oliver Lodge, first Principal of Birmingham University, was associated with Andrew Lang in the Society for Psychical Research – an enthusiasm of Lang's which understandably irritated his colleagues in the Folklore Society. In a sensible paper on 'The Irrationality of War', Lodge referred to antagonism which arises between families, tribes, and eventually nations; 'yet the subdivision of the Race into nations, with differing facilities and a variety of customs and traditions, ought to have a beneficient influence as well as add greatly to the interest of life. So long as the sections co-operate . . . each benefits by the discoveries and advances of the rest, and a valuable spirit of Emulation is achieved.'

Aston Villa's origin a century ago, from among the boys of a Wesleyan Sunday School, suggests an interesting and closely related process. Two years earlier, in 1872, the Primitive Methodist, Joseph Arch, who belonged to the same dissenting tradition prominent in the county, founded the Warwickshire Agricultural Labourers' Union. Warwickshire suffered badly during 18th-century enclosures, and this combined with the claims of England's largest hiring fair at Polesworth to rupture the fabric of traditional country life. The Agricultural Labourers' Union, soon to become a national body, aimed to counter this by improving the social position of the farm labourer. And working-class life in Birmingham and other industrial centres escaped decadence partly because of a sense of social community recreated through organised sport.

Traditional behaviour involved activities in which both town and country could participate. Southam's Godiva procession must have borrowed the idea from Coventry – and the 'black lady' from the 'Indies' was surely the first in an English country spectacle. Popular innovation is often the essence of tradition, though the established classes tend to ignore customs which fall outside the paternal cultural order, especially in an industrialised society. But it is interesting to find George Edmonds, a famous Birmingham radical, inverting the same views (1831): 'Be we, of the working class, never more seen at baby shows, Lord Mayor penny-peeps and gingerbread coronations – be not present as accomplices in such national fooleries. Let the tawdry actors have all the fun to themselves.'

It so happened that the Southam Godiva disappeared soon after, but Edmonds' remarks were evidently ineffective in Coventry. The persistence of tradition, which illustrates an important aspect of human psychology, is, at least in an enlightened society, its own justification.

Roy Palmer, author of this excellent book, is Headmaster of the Dame Elizabeth Cadbury School in Birmingham, and well known for his publications on folk song. He is both a collector and performer, and has also written on folk tale and custom. Not only has he amassed a great deal of valuable material here; he provides interesting insights into its historical and social background.

London University
January 1976

Venetia Newall.

Introduction

Warwickshire has been the subject of many books. Between 1891 and 1910 alone, for example, 115 appeared, many of them guides. The Shakespeare industry has also often turned its attention to the poet's native county. But folklore has been mentioned, if at all, only in passing, and seldom thoroughly explored. Even writers who were interested in folklore only felt able in some cases to devote a small proportion of their books to the subject. Dugdale's classic *Antiquities of Warwickshire,* first published in 1656, is a case in point, valuable though his writing on folklore is.

In other counties, massive contributions to the study of folklore were made by Victorian scholars. One thinks of Harland and Wilkinson in Lancashire, and Charlotte Burne in Shropshire. Unfortunately, there was no monograph of this calibre dealing with Warwickshire, though J. A. Langford's paper, 'Warwickshire folklore and superstitions', which he wrote in 1875 is an excellent piece of work, based on first-hand knowledge of oral traditions. George Morley's *Shakespeare's Greenwood: the Customs of the County* (1900) is perhaps a little light-weight. It tends to adopt the wide-eyed, uncritical approach of the popular guide-book, yet it nevertheless contains a good deal of interesting material, again from first-hand knowledge.

It was not until 1929 that the first, full-length study of Warwickshire folklore by a folklorist appeared. *Folk lore, Old Customs and Superstitions of Shakespeare Land,* was written by J. Harvey Bloom, a clergyman following the eighteenth and nineteenth century tradition of publishing books about his interests. In spite of its slightly suspect title, it is a careful survey, written by a man with a critical awareness of folklore and a deep knowledge both of oral tradition and historical records. One of its limitations is that, like most other writing in this field, it concerns itself almost exclusively with the south of the county, Shakespeare's Warwickshire. The industrial north, the area round Birmingham

11

and Coventry, is barely mentioned.

The present book is the first to appear since Bloom, almost half a century later. Inevitably, it is indebted to him, and to others in the field, such as F. W. Hackwood and Marjorie H. Powis. As well as printed research, the book draws on interviews with many informants, though it is clear that a great deal of work in recording remains to be done. An attempt has been made to cover the industrial and urban lore of the north of the county, though here again there is still ample room for further work.

The first three chapters deal with local traditions of all kinds, and are centred round well-known personalities – Shakespeare, Cromwell, Charles II – and striking events like the Civil War. They also deal with ordinary people and everyday details, lovingly and carefully preserved in tradition: the very hills and fields, the trees and streams, possess their own stories. This visual touch is also apparent in the third chapter in many of the tales of saints and sinners, from St Augustine down to humble men and women,

The ordinary life of people at work and at home provides a background to events and traditions; at the same time it possesses its own customs and folklore. Daily life consisted of beliefs, and maxims, omens and superstitions. It was coloured by the horror of witchcraft and the supernatural. The modern film or play which introduces terror into an everyday situation is often more convincing then a more exotic drama. For many, fear was an ever present reality. 'In the course of my Warwickshire rambles in out-of-the-way localities', wrote A. H. Walls in 1893, 'I have everywhere found amongst the lower classes a lingering belief in the existence of witches, ghosts, and devils.' Perhaps this is no longer true, but it does seem that ghosts at least can still convince many of their power.

The passage rites of marriage, birth and death involved many beliefs and ceremonies. Some have now been discarded, but there is still a strong need in people, which requires that these important events should be marked with the proper ceremonies. Sports and pastimes still hold a strong significance for millions of people. Many of the old sports have disappeared. Some were cruel and violent; in some the spectators were more interesting than the game itself, and the downfall of the sport was caused by the spectators rather than the participants. Perhaps the spectators were seeking the kind of permitted licence, available at fairs and wakes. A safety valve of this kind exists in 'pop' festivals and the like; these respond to a need which society no longer provides for. There are heroes enough in modern society, but none so ascetic as Sir Guy of Warwick, and none – not even the sex-symbols – so alluring and satisfying as Lady Godiva of Coventry.

In working on a survey of this kind, one becomes deeply aware of a process in folklore itself of birth, life, and death, within a continuing tradition. It seems that folklore can be created, or can die, at any time. Dame Alice Croft appears in the fourteenth century, the Dun Cow in the sixteenth, Peeping Tom in the seventeenth. Their stories lived in the mouths and memories of the people. Some no longer do so: they exist only on paper, and must now be said to be dead. Sir Guy, after perhaps a thousand years of life, disappeared, in the middle of the nineteenth century. His story had become irrelevant; it no longer filled a need.

Folklore can also be deliberately killed. A murderous onslaught was mounted in the Puritans in the seventeenth century on customs such as Maying, for example. In the nineteenth century, the main attack was made in the name of mechanisation, work discipline, and good time-keeping. In many large towns, Birmingham especially, fairs were enormously popular long after the industrial revolution. They battled for life, and were ultimately defeated. For these, and other reasons, much of the rich heritage was lost or emasculated or reduced to documents in archives.

The study of folklore today enables us to see it within the context of popular culture and history. Its value lies in making us aware of our roots, of feeling a sense of community and communion. We are made aware that the past is a part of us, and that we are part of the earth. We are made to feel the satisfaction of a culture created by and for a community, rather than for consumption and profit. The time of Shakespeare was by no means perfect, and we could not return to it, even if we wished. Perhaps we may look back in order to plan our way forward.

—▶1◀—

The Heart of England

SHAKESPEARE'S friend, the poet Michael Drayton, wrote of the county in which they were both born as 'That shire which we the heart of England well may call'. Within Warwickshire, several places lay claim to being at the precise centre of England. High Cross, near the intersection of the Fosse Way and Watling Street, was the heart of Roman England. Copston Magna and Meriden both have crosses to support their respective cases, Lillington possesses an oak tree, and Stretton-on-Dunsmore a column. The true centre is apparently at Minworth – which does not trouble to publicise the fact. People living at Acocks Green in Birmingham believe that an oak tree in Arden Road marks the heart of the ancient Forest of Arden, which formerly covered northern Warwickshire so well that a squirrel, or so we are told, could travel from one side of the country to the other without setting foot on the ground.

Arden leads us again to Shakespeare, whose *As you like it*, according to tradition, was set in Hampton-on-Arden. From time to time characters in Shakespeare's plays directly refer to places in Warwickshire. 'Get thee to Coventry', says Falstaff to Bardolph; 'fill me a bottle of sack; our soldiers shall march through. We'll to Sutton Coldfield tonight.' Shakespeare may have known Sutton, for he had relatives there. More important than such isolated references, however, is the poet's deep debt to his county childhood. The very words he used, in some cases, were taken from the dialect he had heard as a boy and a young man; some of them were still being used in Warwickshire, 250 years and more after his death.

They are sturdy, humble words, part of everyday life, at home and at work. Games like loggatts and shovel board are mentioned. There are rural terms such as honey stalks (white clover) and brize (gadfly, pronounced 'breeze') and homely words like quat (pimple), batlet (a wooden beater used for washing clothes) and fardel (faggot). While Shakespeare was acquiring this vocabulary he also became familiar with the popular lore. Indeed, his work is full of it. His fools are in the folk tradition, as are his ghosts and witches. Time after time, he refers to popular beliefs and superstitions, to ballads and sayings, to calendar customs and traditions. One cannot claim that his knowledge of folklore, any more than his vocabulary, came entirely from Warwickshire, but it seems reasonable to argue that his native county at least contributed. In addition to drawing on local lore, he himself became the subject of popular traditions. At Luddington, neither the former church nor its registers survived into recent times, yet tradition stubbornly holds that Shakespeare married Anne Hathaway there. Oddly enough, there is no surviving evidence of the place where his father, John Shakespeare of Snitterfield, married Mary Arden of Wilmcote, but tradition supplies the answer: Aston Cantlow, and adds that the wedding breakfast was held at the King's Head. Shakespeare is said to have studied in a large library at the old moated manor house of Radbrook. The old hall is now a farm house, but there is no trace of a library.

A more spectacular story is that, in about 1585, Shakespeare was caught poaching deer and rabbits from the Clopton and Lucy estates, and had to leave Stratford. He is said to have cooked stolen venison at the Dun Cow inn, near Wilmcote. He was prosecuted, or so we are told, by Sir Thomas Lucy, whose likeness in alabaster may still be seen in the Lucy Chapel of Charlecote Church.

Shakespeare took full revenge. He nailed these verses to the gates of Charlecote Park:

> A Parliament member, a Justice of the Peace,
> At home a poor scarecrow, in London an ass;
> If lousy is Lucy, as some folk miscall it,
> Then Lucy is lousy, whatever befall it.
> > He thinks himself great,
> > Yet an ass in his state
> > We allow by his ears
> > With but asses to mate.

Later he composed a satirical ballad which circulated orally until 1690, when the Professor of Greek at Cambridge was passing through Stratford, and heard an old women singing it at in inn. 'Such was his respect for Mr Shakespeare's genius', wrote the eighteenth century diarist, John Byng, 'that he gave her a new gown, for the following two stanzas; and could she have said it all, he would have given her ten guineas.

> Sir Thomas was too covetous
> To covet so much deer;
> When horns enough upon his head
> Most plainly did appear.
> Had not his worship one deer left,
> What then, he had a wife
> Took pains enough to find him horns
> Should hold him during life.'

Finally, Shakespeare is said to have caricatured Sir Thomas Lucy as Mr Justice Shallow in *Henry IV* and *The Merry Wives of Windsor*.

Commentators have frequently tried to undermine these traditional beliefs. We are told that there were no deer in Charlecote Park in Shakespeare's time; that the old woman's ballad was a forgery; that Shallow was really William Gardiner, and not Thomas Lucy. An entire book was written to support the last contention. But these scholarly efforts have made little impact on the stories, which operate on a different level. In the copy of *Merry Wives* at Charlecote House, the opening scene with Shallow has been physically cut out. The Lucy family at least believed the story.

More tangible evidence of Shakespeare's misdeeds was marked on the first Ordnance Survey map, published in 1831, where 'Shakespeare's Crab' was indicated, just out of Bidford on the road to Stratford. Bidford was renowned for its drinking men, and had two teams, the Topers and the Sippers, which challenged the men of other towns and villages. On one occasion the Topers were playing away, so to speak, while the Sippers were at home, entertaining a team from Stratford, which included Shakespeare. They met at the Falcon Inn: when the Stratford men later left for home, they were much the worse for wear. They got no further than a crab apple tree, just outside the town, and spent the night under its branches. The following morning Shakespeare declined an invitation to renew the contest, and trudged home in disgust. He is then said to have made up this rhyme about Bidford and its neighbours:

Piping Pebworth, dancing Marston,
Haunted Hillborough, and hungry Grafton;
With dodging Exhall, Papist Wixford,
Beggarly Broom, and drunken Bidford.

Pebworth, now three-quarters of a mile into Worcestershire, was known for its morris dancers, who were accompanied by the pipe and tabor. It has a further association with Shakespeare: its main street is said to be called Friday Street because Shakespeare went to drink there on Fridays. He attracted so many people to hear and join in his conversation that the street became very busy on those days. Marston, now Long Marston, had a famous 'band of morris dancers who were wont to attend the wakes, fairs, and merry makings for many miles around'. Hillborough had a number of gloomy associations. There is a field called Palmer's Piece which was haunted by the ghost of the man gibbetted there on Good Friday 1801 for murdering his wife. One story says that he drowned her in the Avon; another that he poisoned her. The manor house at Hillborough also has the reputation of being haunted. A former occupant believes that the ghost is Shakespeare's 'other Anne', the mysterious Anne Whateley. Within the last few years, an architect working late in the house on drawings for alterations found a mysterious figure at his elbow. Grafton, now Temple

Grafton, had poor soil, which made it difficult to earn a living there. The description of Exhall is harder to explain. It may mean possessing obscure by-ways, or heavy land, or merely being sulky ('dudging'). The Throckmortons, a well-known Catholic family, once owned land at Wixford, and Broom was originally a hamlet of squatters on the heath, hence the word beggarly.

Many similar rhymes about other parts of the county, have not been attributed to Shakespeare. They were an art form and a poor man's Baedeker, providing sometimes-dubious information. Sutton Coldfield produced sheep, and Tamworth had horned cattle. Birmingham was noted for its love of rough sports, and Coleshill was notorious for poachers and hen-roost robbers, all faithfully reflected in the rhyme:

> Sutton for mutton, and Tamworth for beeves;
> Brummagem for blackguards, Coleshill for thieves.

The second line sometimes read:

> Walsall for bandylegs [or knock-knees], and Brummagem for thieves;

or:

> Yenton [Erdington] for a pretty girl, and Brummagem for thieves.

The speaker's point of view was obviously important. Local partisanship dictated some of the adjectives. Another rhyme, about more villages near Stratford, is very unflattering:

> Daft Dorsington, lousy Luddington,
> Welford for witches, Binton for bitches,
> An' Weston at th' end of th' 'orld.

This is echoed by:

> Silhill [Solihull] on the hill, Balsall in the hole,
> Beggarly Barston and lousy Knowle.

Sometimes the adjectives run out, and the rhyme becomes a list of names:

> Dirty Gritton, dingy Greet,
> Beggarly Winchcombe, Sudeley sweet;
> Hartshorn and Whittington Bell,
> Andoversford and merry Frog Mill.

The rhymes sometimes have a poetic quality, though this one has a sting in the tail:

> There's Biterscote and Bonehill, and Dunstal upon Dunn,
> Hopwas and Coaton, and miry Wigginton;
> Little Armington and Great Armington, with Wovil houses
>   [nearby,
> Glascote and Wilncote, and merry Fazeley;
> Comberford and Lyerscote, and Bole Hall street,
> And Tamworth is the head town where all the cuckolds meet.

Some of these assertions are impossible to check, but this one has a ring of truth about it:

> Idlicote on the hill, Whatcote downderry,
> Beggarly Oxhill and lousy Fulready;
> Yawning Yettington, peeping Pillerton,
> And one-eyed Marston.

It is said that the tag about Clifton is based on fact:

> Clifton-upon-Dunsmore, in Warwickshire,
> Sold the church Bible to buy a bear.

Finally, another splendidly boastful piece of local patriotism:

> The Armscot boys are very good boys,
> The Nobold [Newbold] boys are better;
> The Halford boys can stand on one leg
> And kick them all in the gutter.

In addition to rhymes, there are set phrases about some places. 'Hungry Harborne, poor and proud', was one. Henley people were said to remark 'More fools in Henley' whenever they saw strangers, but it was apparently turned against them. 'Fast and true, like Coventry blue' is the ancestor of the well-known phrase, 'true blue'. Coventry blue was dye used for the ribbons produced in the town. They were a favourite purchase at country fairs, until the industry collapsed under foreign competition in the 1870s. The expression 'sent to Coventry' is said to have originated during the Civil War. At that time, unlike most of its neighbours, Coventry was a walled town. Royalist prisoners, from Birmingham for example, were sent to Coventry for safe keeping. There might well have been some truth in the story. Certainly the walls of Coventry were levelled at the Restoration, on the orders of Charles II.

The Civil War left its mark on local tradition for many centuries. There is a story that when General Ireton was staying at Packwood House in 1642 he saw a young man lurking in the grounds, a cavalier who was courting his daughter. Ireton had him taken to Kenilworth Castle, and shot. This is clearly not a contemporary story, since Ireton was not married until 1646, and Kenilworth was not in parliamentary hands in 1642. But there could well be historical truth in the story that Cromwell, then a captain of horse, climbed the tower of the church at Burton Dassett to view the progress of the battle at Edgehill. In his haste to rejoin the fighting he is said to have slid down one of the bell-ropes.

The dead at Edgehill were buried by a copse of fir trees at what is now called Battle Farm, and at another spot, still known as Gravefields. On the first Christmas Eve after the battle, shepherds on the hill saw ghostly armies fighting through the night, till dawn. A magistrate and a parson went the following evening and saw the apparitions, as did 'six gentlemen of credit' sent by Charles I from Oxford. A pamphlet describing the ghostly battle, entitled *A great wonder in heaven*, was published shortly afterwards, in January 1643. There is no record of any subsequent appearance, although watches have been kept on the hill from time to time, on Christmas Eve.

After the battle, a certain Jeremiah Stone, who was a corporal of dragoons, went to Warwick with a bag of money he had looted from the dead. He was wounded, and, while he was recovering at the Anchor Inn, he entrusted his money to the landlady. When he was well again he asked for his property back, but his hosts denied all knowledge of it, and threw him out. The soldier drew his sword and tried to break down the door, but the landlord had him arrested. While Stone was in prison awaiting trial for attempted breaking and entering, the devil came and offered help, in exchange for his soul. The soldier refused, but the devil told him to ask for an attorney when he came before the bench, and to choose the man wearing a red cap and feather. The soldier took his advice, but his attorney was in fact the devil. In his defence, the lawyer suggested that the inn should be searched to see if the money was there. The landlord denied possessing it, and wished that the devil might take him if he told a lie. The devil took him at his word, 'seized upon his body and carried him over the Market Place, [with] nothing left behind but a terrible stinke'. The story is related in a pamphlet of 1642, which states: 'This is the truth, John Finch (a shoomaker) in Saint Martin's, being an eye-witnesse doth testifie the same'. The tale survived in oral tradition until this century, with the variation that the devil became a red-capped juryman.

Other Warwickshire traditions of the Civil War deal with a pleasanter subject – the escape of Charles II. After the battle at Worcester and his flight to Boscobel, he set out disguised as Will Jackson, servant to Mistress Lane. At Erdington near Birmingham, he had to stop for his horse to be shod. The blacksmith supported Parliament, and Charles felt that it would be wise to agree with his views. The blacksmith complimented him on 'speaking like an honest man'. Jane Lane later married Sir Clement Fisher, of Packington, where she subsequently died and was buried.

Still disguised as a servant, Charles stopped at a house in Long Marston, which has kept the name of King's Lodge. To maintain his anonymity, he was obliged to work in the kitchen. The cook, enraged at his clumsiness, hit him, just as Parliamentary troopers came in, and they did not for a moment suspect him of being the king. He was able to ride on through Snitterfield Bushes to Bishopton Flat, and make good his escape. The road through the woods is still called King's Lane.

Scenes of violent death in the Civil War also lived on; indeed, they still do. A headless ghost has been seen in Tyburn Road, Birmingham, near the old Tyburn Inn, at a place where soldiers 'shot a lad who could not speak and tell them what they wanted to know. After he was shot they cut off his head. His body was thrown into what is now Pype Hayes Park and the head was carried on a pole to a place called New Shipston. The ghost was seen near the seats opposite the Old Tyburn Inn, and a similar one has been sighted at New Shipston'. Another, even more spectacular, supernatural story from the Civil War also comes from Birmingham. It is told by Mr Tom Langley, who joined the police in 1927, and was first stationed at Digbeth.

About two o'clock in the morning I was in Fazeley Street talking to the sergeant. It was a cold night and, of course, apart from the occasional noise from the railway, very quiet. Suddenly there was a terrible scream. It seemed to come from the direction of Milk Street. It was spine chilling. It crescendoed for some seconds and then stopped suddenly. I can only liken it to the shriek I once heard when a cat was killed by a fox; this was also in the night.

I said to the sergeant, 'Somebody's been killed.' I expected him to move quickly, even if it was only in the wrong direction. He stood still, and said, 'You will hear that again if you work this beat long enough. Put it down to an engine in the sidings. Some of the old Brums round here say it's a ghost, but we are paid to catch thieves, not ghosts.'

I took the sergeant's advice, put it down to a railway engine, and forgot all about it. Two years or so later I was on the beat again and heard it. I knew at this second experience it was not an engine, and I decided to make quiet enquiries. I mentioned it to an uncle who had been retired from the Force for several years and had been on the Division in 1895. He told me he had heard it several times during his twenty-five years' service, but it was better to forget it. I was still not satisfied.

Now it happened that in a factory in Allison Street was a night watchman. He was a pensioner, over seventy years of age. He had joined the Force in 1880, and his father had been a policeman in the district in the 1850s. This man, by the way, was one of the best-read men I have ever met. He was always awake and always reading. He is the only man I have ever known who had read *War and Peace* from start to finish and enjoyed it. I spoke about this scream to him and he told me this story.

When Prince Rupert sacked Birmingham during the Civil War in 1643, the town was mainly round the River Rea in the Digbeth area. The inhabitants knew that the Royalists were quartered on Camp Hill, and practically all of them left the area and hid in the fields of Edgbaston and Winson Heath. One man, named Moore, with his wife and five children, lived in a cottage in Milk Street, and for some reason stayed put. Three of Rupert's troopers dragged the family into Digbeth, and one of them beheaded the father, mother, and the children. The last to be murdered was a girl of thirteen. She saw all her family mercilessly slaughtered, and just before it happened to her, she screamed. It was his opinion that the girl's last terrible cry was still echoing down the arches of the years.

The old cottage was demolished just after the second World War, and, so far as I know, the scream has not been heard for forty years. Moore's Row is still there, between Milk Street and Floodgate Street.

— 2 —

A Local
Habitation

CHARLES II is not the only monarch linked with places in Warwickshire. Ethelbald, King of Mercia from 716 to 757, is said to have been murdered by Saxon nobles at Seckington. King John is traditionally associated with a castle which once stood on a hill at the west end of Kineton. A well at the foot of the hill is still called King John's Well. Three miles out of Warwick on the Kenilworth road Blacklow Hill, otherwise known as Gaveston's Mount, was the reputed place of execution of Piers Gaveston, the favourite of Edward II. He was captured in 1312 by Guy, Earl of Warwick, who declared before executing him: 'The Black Dog of Arden is come to keep his oath that you should one day feel his teeth.' The Black Dog Inn at Southam has a sign which shows a knight in armour; a second knight in the background is being executed. At Astley a memorial in a field marks the traditional spot where 'formerly stood a huge hollow oak tree in which Henry Grey, Duke of Suffolk, Lord of the Manor of Astley, the father of Lady Jane Grey, took refuge from his pursuers. He was betrayed here by his

24

keeper, Underwood, and executed on Tower Hill'. This was in 1554.

Many local traditions concern humbler people. Hampton Field was the meeting place in 1607 of the Warwickshire diggers who had joined the rising directed against 'those late enclosures, which made them of ye poorest sort reddy to pyne 'with want'. The Warwickshire men complained that the 'incroaching Tirants' had 'depopulated and overthrowne whole townes and made thereof sheep pastures' and argued that it was better to die manfully than 'to be pined to death for want of y' wch those devouring encroachers do serve theyr fatt hogges and sheep withall'. The diggers had a semi-mythical leader, Captain Pouch, whose name derived from his supposedly magic pouch. He also claimed divine inspiration. The rising was nevertheless put down 'by martiall execution and civill justice'.

Later enclosures – in the eighteenth century – led to the destruction of the Red Horse, near Tysoe. Sir Thomas Dugdale saw and described it in the seventeenth century: 'There is a cut upon the side of Edg-Hill the Proportion of a Horse, in a very large Forme; which, by Reason of the Ruddy Colour of the Earth, is called the Red Horse, and giveth Denomination to that fruitfull and pleasant Countrey thereabouts, commonly called the Vale of the Red Horse.' The tradition was that the horse had been cut to commemorate the conduct (or the horse) of Richard Nevil, Earl of Warwick. At the battle of Towton in 1461 he had declared that he wished to fight on equal terms with his men, whereupon he dismounted and killed his horse with his sword. It seems likely that the Red Horse was older than that. Perhaps there was a scouring soon after the battle, hence the association. At all events, the scouring – that is to say, the removal of weeds and grass – took place every year, attended by tremendous festivities, on Palm Sunday. In 1798 the enclosure of the hill put an end to the tradition, and the area became private land. The owners of the Sunrising Inn at Tysoe kept things going for a few years by cutting their own horse in a nearby meadow, but the old ceremony never revived.

No doubt at least partly from commercial motives, innkeepers were, and are, great keepers of traditions. The oldest pub in Warwickshire, dating from 1306, is the Green Man at Erdington – now called the Lad in the Lane. The earlier name is a powerful reminder of ancient beliefs. The Ivy Bush, another name which occurs several times in the county is a plant which was sacred to Bacchus. The Four Crosses Inn at Willoughby was the Three Crosses until the eighteenth century when Jonathan Swift spent a night there. He left this scratched on his bedroom window the following morning:

> There are three crosses at your door:
> Hang up your wife and you'll count four.

The Four Alls at Welford is named from:

> A king who rules over all; a parson who prays for all;
> A soldier who fights for all; and a farmer who pays for all.

The Roebuck at Priors Marston, now a private house, was known locally in the eighteenth century as Rogues' Hall, when it was used as their headquarters by bands of robbers who preyed on drovers. The old Welsh Road left the A5 at Brownhills and passed through Kenilworth and Southam on its way to London. Drovers brought herds of cattle along it and returned home the same way with the proceeds from their sales. A highwayman called Bendigo Mitchell is said to have slept in the Old Inn – again, now a private house – at Bishop's Tachbrook. His territory was the Fosse Way east of Moreton Morrell. Together with a companion, he was hanged at Warwick in 1772. Another highwayman, captured at an inn at Warwick is said to have committed suicide in order to escape hanging. His horse had an enchanted bridle so he could not be caught; presumably he was dismounted when he was taken. Like many of his kind, he claimed to rob the rich, and give to the poor. The bulk of his treasure was not recovered. It is said to lie in a field called the Hen and Chickens at Fenny Compton.

In a farm at Meriden still called Highwayman's House, there is an underground stable – presumably a former hide-out. On the road from Daventry to Dunchurch, between the Cold Comfort and the Blue Boar, a highwayman robbed a Mr Leigh in 1747. His description of the robber has survived: 'well mounted upon a Bay Mare, and had under him a new Pair of Leather [saddle] Bags. He was a middle-sized Man, pitted very much with the Small Pox, and had on under his Hat a woollen Cap, but no Boots nor Spurs, and seem'd to be about twenty-three years of Age.' At about the same time, or a little later, footpads stopped a coach in the Warwick Road at Knowle, killed the driver, and robbed the passengers. For many years afterwards the driver's ghost was seen about the fields on moonlight nights. A possible appearance as late as 1918 was traced to a young errand boy who happened to be passing. Nevertheless, it is interesting that such a mistake could have been made, at so late a date.

A John Smith, Senior, was executed for highway robbery at Gaydon, near Kineton, in 1787. Two years later, John Smith, Junior, was executed for the same crime. A young woman recovered his body and carried it away on a donkey from Warwick, where the execution took place, to Culworth, where it was buried. The younger John Smith was fortunate, since the bodies of those executed were often gibbeted and placed by the roadside to deter others, a practice which was not abolished until 1834. For this reason, there are several Gibbet Hills in Warwickshire. The one near Stoneleigh marks the site of the gallows where three murderers' bodies were chained up in 1765. Another, six miles north of Rugby where the Lutterworth road crosses the Watling Street, was where William Banbury was murdered in 1676, and one of his assailants gibbeted at the scene of the crime. A nearby field is called Dead Man's Corner. There was yet another on the Chester Road, near Birmingham, where Oscott College now stands. A man who robbed a London mercer at that spot was first hanged, then gibbeted there, in 1729. Gallows Hill Farm, near Whichford, is where thieves were executed who preyed on drovers using a green road nearby. The road is still called Traitors' Ford Lane.

Near Wolvey is a little mound where Lady Dorothy Smythe is said to have been burnt at the stake in 1555 for causing the death of her husband. Sir Thomas Holte was another aristocratic criminal – according to popular tradition, at any rate. His home, Aston Hall, still stands, but the story goes that at Duddeston Hall, his previous seat, he murdered his cook by cleaving his skull with a hatchet. This happened in 1606. The unfortunate cook is said to have been buried in the cellar, and, when the house at Duddeston was demolished in 1850, there was considerable local speculation as to whether his remains would come to light. They did not. The red hand in the

Holte arms, which can be seen in Aston Church, is supposed to commemorate this evil deed. The story was evidently circulating during Sir Thomas' lifetime, for he brought and won a libel action over it. The red hand of Ulster appeared in the arms of all Barons Patent after 1611, by decree of James I, and not for any infamous reason. But the popular tradition remained.

There are less unpleasant reminders of our Warwickshire ancestors' crimes. The saying, 'If you don't mind what you're about, you'll get over Moulden's Bridge' means, 'You'll go to the bad'. It recalls the name of the bridge over which prisoners passed to Warwick gaol and assizes. A ducking stool has been preserved in the crypt of St Mary's, Warwick. There are still stocks at a number of villages, including Shuckbrugh, Haselor. Dunchurch and Loxley (where they have been put in the church). At Henley they were taken down in 1793, but at Knowle they survived until the end of the nineteenth century. At Rugby the stocks were in frequent use in 1838 'when the construction of the London and Birmingham Railway was being carried on. Navvies, who little respected the decencies of civilised society, were here confined, and derisively termed *children in the wood.*' At Coleshill, a pillory, stocks, and whipping post all survive. At Berkswell there is a set of stocks on the village green with five sockets for feet. The local explanation is that they were made to accommodate a one-legged old soldier and his two companions. They were apparently fond of drink, which is why they were often in the stocks.

Stories are attached to individual fields, streams, trees, even stones. To the north of Stockton village is a block of stone kept in a railed-off area. It is said to have been carried by the waters from Mount Sorrel in Leicestershire at the time of the Flood. A plot of land at Barcheston, the site of a former village, is called Old Town. The local story is that the village was knocked down by Cromwell. A field at Bulkington, known as the Churl's Piece, has its own history. One of the Lord Zouches, who lived at Weston-in-Arden, wished to add a meadow to his estate. He invited all the freeholders to his house and asked them to sell him their joint property. They all agreed, except for one Rogers, whose refusal so incensed his lordship that he said: 'Let the churl alone with his piece.' Hence the name. Child's Oak is a tree near Berkswell — so called because a boy bled to death in its hollow. The children were playing pig and butcher, and the make-believe butcher used a real knife, with tragic effect. On the road between Bidford and Wixford stood St George's Elm. According to tradition, St George was buried beneath it and the tree grew from an elm stake driven through his body. The tree was supposed to bleed if its bark was cut.

Near Compton Verney, where the Fosse Way is crossed by the Wellesbourne to Kineton road, there is a massive oak and a wood, called Bowshot Wood. The tale is that two local men each owned land which the other wished to add to his estate. Eventually one of them agreed to exchange some property for a Talbot sporting dog. The amount would be the square of the distance the man could shoot an arrow along the Fosse. He shot, and the arrow would have gone far, but it stuck in the oak. Bowshot Wood is the name of the land he acquired.

Hirons' Hole at Littleham Bridge is called after William Hirons, who was killed and robbed there in 1820 by four men named Quiney, Adams, Sidney and Heytrey. They were hanged at Warwick in April 1821, and Hirons is commemorated by a monument in Alveston Church. It is said that he was found the morning after the murder with his head in a hole, which no one has ever been able to fill in since. More cheerfully, Whittington Cottage, near the vicarage at Long Compton, is said to be the birthplace of Dick Whittington.

Brooks and wells often possess their own traditions. King John's Well at Kineton has already been mentioned. In Sutton Park a spring, called Rowton Well, was once thought to possess medicinal properties. The Keeper's Well traditionally takes its name from John Holt, the keeper of the park in the reign of Edward IV. Another well, at the south-west end of Bracebridge Pool, is called St Mary's or Druid's Well. Sutton is said once to have been the seat of the arch-druid of Britain; perhaps this was his well, which was later christianised. Chad Valley, between Harborne and Edgbaston, was known as Good Knaves' End and before that as Hungry Valley. A spring there could foretell the future: 'when it betokenethe batayle it rennys foule and trouble water, and when betoken the derthe or pestylence it rennyth as clere as any watere'. Neither alternative is very attractive, but presumably dearth and pestilence are preferable to battle. In the early nineteenth century a spring at Allesley, Dudley's Spring, and a similar one at Atherstone, indicated the future price of corn. To the east of the county, near Watling Street, Sketchley Well is said to have sharpened the wits of those who tasted its water. 'He has been to Sketchley' was said of a man who was mentally spry. Near Dunchurch there is a little stream called Rainsbrook. Tradition says that there will one day be a great battle, and the stream will flow with blood. Three kings will be present, their horses held by a miller with three thumbs. So far, this rather unlikely set of circumstances has not occurred. Hob's Hole, a Coventry well, had its own mayor who was elected annually: 'the forcible ducking of his worship' ended the ceremony.

In a piece of woodland between Oversley Wood and Haselor there is a conical hill known as Alcock's Arbour. Dugdale wrote down its story in the seventeenth century, and it is still told today in much the same manner:

> Southwards from Haselor (but within the same parish) is a coppice wood, and in it a notable hill, which is of such a steep and equal ascent from every side as if it has been artificially made, so that it is a very eminent mark over all that part of the country, and by the common people called Alcock's Arbour; towards the foot whereof is a hole; now almost filled up, having been the entrance into a cave, as the inhabitants report. Of which cave there is an old wives' story, that passes for current amongst the people of the adjacent towns, viz., that one Alcock, a great robber, used to lodge therein, and having got much money by that course of life, hid it in an iron-bound chest, whereunto were three keys: which chest they say is still there, but guarded by a cock that continually sits upon it. And that one time an Oxford scholar came thither with a key that opened two of the locks, but as he was attempting to open the third the cock seized on him. To all which they add that, if bone of the party who set the cock there could be brought, he would yield up the chest.

A similar story is told of another hill, the Mound, near Lindley Hall. In this case, the robber was Dick Turpin.

People knew and loved their surroundings, and took a fierce pride in them. A remarkable example of inter-village rivalry exists between Ilmington in Warwickshire and Ebrington, just over the hill in Gloucestershire. The Ilmington people assert that an

Ebrington woman (alternatively pronounced as Yebberton or Yubberton) put a pig on the wall to watch the band go by. Other villagers saw the full moon shining through the branches of an 'ellum' tree, and thought it was a cheese. They heaped up all the tables and chairs in the village in order to reach it, but, not having enough, they removed the ones at the bottom and put them on top to make the pile higher. There are other stories about the church with its squat little tower. The parishioners held a meeting to decide what colour the building should be whitewashed. They also manured the tower to make it grow higher. They would have preferred the church on top of the hill, so all the men decided to get together and put it into position. 'The parson sez, "Put yer coats down on the top side and then you can see how far you ha' pushed it". This is what they did; then they went round and shoved. Meanwhile an old tramp stole their coats, so when they came round again to see how far they had pushed it, they sez, "Damned if us haven't pushed it atop of our coats".' Some of the stories at the expense of the Yebberton mawms [fools] were put into verse, and sung to the tune of 'Dumble dum dairy'.

A Yebberton mawm to Campden went,
To buy a wheelbarrow was his intent;
He carried the barrow from town to town
For fear the wheel should be bruised by the ground.
Chorus
Sing dumble dum dairy, flare up Mary, oh what wonderful times.

There was a mad dog come through the town
And bit the side of the barrow all round;
They took it to the sea to be dipped
And swore the dog he should be whipped.

Old Tommy ——— to show he was no fool
Built a big hovel over the pool;
Somebody asked him the reason why:
It was for his ducks to swim in the dry.

They mucked the church tower to make it grow high
But not so lofty as the sky;
And when the muck began to sink
They swore the tower had grown an inch.

One moonlight night when it did freeze
The moon shone in a pool – they thought it was a cheese;
They fetched some rakes to rake it out
And swore they couldn't get it out.

Now Mrs Morris got up to brew;
There was summat the matter with the chimbley flue.
Master Morris got up to see
A donkey's legs down his chimbley.

The donkey was stuck in the chimbley top
·And his tail behind went flipperty flop.
The donkey belonged to Benjamin Harris
And they took him to Moreton to swear his parish.

The Yebberton mawms to show their power
Lit a fire on top of the church tower.
The lead ran down like blood from a slaughter;
The old women ran to catch the soft water.

So much for Ilimington's view of its neighbours. Ebrington's reply
has not been recorded.

—⊃ 3 ⊂—

Saints and
Sinners

THERE ARE portraits of four Saxon bishops in the east window of Snitterfield Church: Dunstan, Wolfstan, Oswald and Edwin. The miracle worker, St Wulfstan, is said to have been born in Warwickshire. Yardley Church is dedicated to St Edburgha, King Alfred's grand-daughter, and her remains are said to lie under the altar. Her father and three brothers were all kings, and her six sisters married princes, and yet she worked as a servant. She already showed her piety at the age of four. Her father offered her the Gospels, a chalice and a handful of jewels: she took the holy book in one hand and the vessel in the other. When Edburgha was abbess at Pershore she stayed up at night to wash the nuns' garments while they slept. She was originally buried at Winchester, then transferred to Pershore, and finally laid to rest at Yardley.

St George is traditionally held to have been born and died at Coventry, though at least one other place in the county claims to be his resting place. He appears in church windows at Baddesley Clinton and Bubbenhall. His female counterpart, St Margaret, is shown slaying a dragon at Mancetter. In a number of churches St George is linked with St Nicholas. At Berkswell there are kneeling effigies of both, and at Beaudesert they share a window. Here, St Nicholas, the original Santa Claus, shelters a tubful of children with his cloak. At Ladbroke he is shown with three children and three bags of money. At Willoughby he is depicted as Bishop of Myra, with a ship and on its sail another picture of the three children he saved from frying. It will be remembered that a rascally innkeeper killed them and salted them down. St Nicholas restored them to life. There are also the three money bags in which he took gifts of gold to a poor man as dowries for his daughters – the origin of giving presents at Christmas.

A recumbent effigy in the south porch of the church at Long Compton is said to represent St Augustine himself. He came to the village in 404 to preach the gospel. The parish priest complained that the lord of the manor refused to pay his tithes and St Augustine confronted him when he came to church. The lord still refused to pay so St Augustine excommunicated him at once. He added from the altar: 'I command that no excommunicated person be present at mass'. At these words a dead man who lay buried in the church rose from his grave and politely stood outside till mass was over. St Augustine questioned him and found that he was a former patron of the church who had refused to pay tithes, died, and 'been thrust into hell'. He pointed out the grave of the priest who had excommunicated him and, at the request of the saint, the priest rose from his grave, confirmed the story, and denounced the man as a sinner. Augustine took pity on him, presented him with a scourge, and granted him absolution. At the saint's command, he returned to his grave, and fell into dust. Augustine then offered to allow the priest, who had been dead for 150 years, to return to earth. But the priest begged him not to disturb his rest by bringing him back to the troubles of earthly life. Augustine allowed him to return to his grave and he, too, immediately fell into dust. It is not surprising that, after this demonstration, the gentleman changed his mind about paying tithes. Others listening to this story would no doubt feel the same way.

St Edith also stood up for the prerogatives of the church. After the Norman conquest, Sir Robert de Marmion, Lord of Tamworth, expelled the nuns from their convent at Polesworth, St Edith among them. She was a Saxon princess of the royal blood who had married the King of Northumbria in order to win him for Christianity. She had failed to do this, but preserved her virginity — perhaps the two were connected — and retired to Polesworth Abbey. After the expulsion she appeared to Marmion in a dream and smote him with her crozier. He took the hint, and restored the nuns to their abbey, where they remained until the time of Henry VIII, who was apparently made of sterner stuff than Marmion.

Another Warwickshire miracle involved Sir Hugh de Hatton. He was captured by infidels while away on a crusade in the Middle East, and imprisoned. He prayed to St Leonard, the patron of prisoners, and was transported to the Forest of Arden. His wife either failed or refused to recognise him until he produced his half of a ring which they had broken together. Such broken tokens were often used when absences were long and communications slow. In gratitude for his deliverance, Sir Hugh founded a house of Benedictine nuns, which was built on the spot where the meeting with his wife took place. The abbey church, which still exists, was dedicated to St Leonard.

One of the nuns at Wroxall — Sir Hugh's abbey — was called Alice Croft or Craft. She had a dream that the Virgin Mary asked her to build a Lady Chapel by the church. When she ignored it, the dream was repeated: 'came the same voice to her againe, and gave her the same charge more sharplye'. Alice still delayed, so the Virgin appeared in person and reprimanded her. Alice then went to the prioress and explained that she only possessed fifteen pence. The prioress encouraged her to be bold, saying that 'our Lady would encrease her store', so Alice arranged for some masons to start work as soon as possible. When they arrived, although it was harvest time, they found an area by the church covered in snow and the chapel was accordingly built on this site. Every week until the chapel was completed Alice found enough money lying on the ground in the churchyard to pay for the work of the masons and their materials.

At Knowle, surprisingly, the site of the church was chosen by fairies. Building work was begun on the hill above St Anne's Well, but fairies came every night and removed the stones to the present site, until the masons took the hint and built in the new place. Conversely, at Warmington work began on the village green and fairies carried the materials to the present site of the church, about 150 feet higher up.

A twelfth-century Cistercian Abbey at Merevale was a place of pilgrimage because of its image of the Virgin, until the pilgrims brought the plague, in 1361. Little remains of the abbey now, but the gate chapel has been preserved as part of the parish church. At Honiley, St John's Well to the north of the church is also said to have been a place of pilgrimage. Offchurch takes its name from Offa, King of Mercia, who died in 796. A stone in the outside of the north wall of the nave is said to be the lid of his coffin, implying that his bones lie under the wall. It would normally be unusual for a King to be buried on the north side of a church, which was considered an unlucky and unfortunate site, reserved for criminals and paupers. Military executions during the Civil War took place on the north side of some churches — at Wootton Wawen, Kenilworth and Stratford, for example. In Wroxall Abbey Church, as in some others, there is a door in the north wall called the Devil's Door. Now walled up, it used to be opened just for baptisms and exorcisms, to give the devil a chance to leave by a private exit so that he would not meet anyone coming into the church.

At the entrance to Baddesley Clinton Church the visitor steps on a mat covering the gravestone of Nicholas Broome, who requested in his will 'that my body may be buried within the parish church of Baddesley Clinton, where as many people may tread upon me when they come into the church'. This was a part of his penance for two murders. He killed John Herthill, who had murdered Broome's father near Barford. In the violence of the late fifteenth and early sixteenth centuries, this might have been regarded as excusable, but Broome then murdered a priest,whom he found 'chokking his wife under the chin'. In order to obtain a pardon from the Pope, Broome had to pay for a steeple to be added to the church at Baddesley, and for three bells and possibly a new tower at Packwood.

In the Beauchamp Chapel at St Mary's, Warwick, the central monument is the effigy of Richard Beauchamp, Earl of Warwick, who died at Rouen in 1439 and was brought home to be buried. There is a story that, two hundred years later the floor of the chapel collapsed to reveal Richard's body intact for a moment only, before it crumbled to dust. Perhaps the hair remained, for another tale says that the women of Warwick twisted it into rings.

The marble busts in Sutton Church of Henry Pudsey and his wife preserve a story of passionate love. When Henry died there was a scandal when his widow married William Wilson, the mason who made the busts. She obtained a knighthood for him, and when she died he returned to his former trade. In his old age he made plans to be buried beside her, but the relatives refused to admit him to the Pudsey family vault. This was why he bought a piece of land adjacent to it, in which to be buried, consoling himself with the thought: 'There will only be a wall between us, and as I am a mason there will be no trouble in cutting my way through.' One feels he would have agreed with this inscription in the church porch at Wolverton:

That thou injure no man, dove-like be;
And serpent-like, that no man injure thee.

Misericords, also at Wolverton, include St George. At Middleton there is a Green Man carved on the oak chancel screen. Elsewhere, there are several musical carvings. At Grendon the altar rails have four figures in relief – one is blowing a bagpipe and another a flute. In the Beauchamp Chapel at Warwick there are angels in painted glass of the fifteenth century playing harps, violins, organs, pipes, bagpipes – and musical glasses. A piece of written music is also represented. Music was provided in churches by groups of local musicians. At Hampton-in-Arden, for example, a band played in the west gallery until 1839, when the organ was installed.

The most powerful form of music in church was provided by the bells, which served to regulate the community on a daily, weekly, and even seasonal basis. At Brailes there was a daily bell at 6 a.m., and another at Honington at 9 a.m. In large towns like Warwick and Coventry and in smaller ones like Knowle, Nuneaton, Rugby, and Stratford : and indeed, no doubt, elsewhere – the old curfew bell still sounded every day at 8 p.m. As well as ringing for morning service on Sundays at Kineton, a bell sounded afterwards to show that it was time for the puddings to be cooled, hence its name – the Pudding Bell. At Barcheston the church had only three bells, and their chimes were supposed to say:

Pitchpole Jack, Pitchpole Jack,

One-a-penny, two-a-penny,
Pitchpole Jack.

On New Year's Day churches throughout the county used to ring the Devil's Peal. This involved as many strokes on a bell as there were years since the advent of Christ. On Shrove Tuesday the Pancake bell was rung in the north of the county at 11 a.m. and at noon in the south. Places where this happened include Tredington, Bidford, Aston Cantlow, Allesley, Bedworth, Clifton, Coventry, Grandborough, Rugby, Sutton Coldfield and Shipston-on-Stour. The bell was originally a summons to the faithful to go and be shriven; later it was supposed to say 'The pan's a-burning, the pan's a-burning', At Ilmington it was a signal for the parish clerk to set out on his yearly visit to the farms to collect the pancakes which were his due. He and five bell-ringers carried them in a large basket lined with flannel, singing 'Link it, lank it, gi'e me a pankit'. An observer sadly noted in 1896 that 'The custom of ringing this bell is falling into disuse'.

Bell-ringing was also at one time very common in Warwickshire on Bonfire Night. Ansley, Bidford, Bilton, Fenny Compton, Grendon, Ilmington, Lapworth, Middleston, Shotteswell, Tachbrook and Wormleighton were among the places which kept up this custom. At Solihull the bells were rung and a dole was distributed on All Souls' Day (2 November). On St Thomas' Day (21 December) some villages – Ettington, Bidford, Fenny Compton, Frankton, Harbury, Kinston, Tachbrook, Southam and Wellesbourne – sounded a bell at 6 a.m. which was the signal for Thomasing to begin.

When new bells were raised in a church there was often a celebration in the village. There was one at King's Norton, remembered in the song:

> Such ringing ne'er was known before:
> They fairly shook the spire;
> They kicked up one continuous roar,
> 'Twas slam round, change and fire.
> The guns did shoot and folks did hoot
> On hearing such a clatter;
> They ran about to see the rout
> And learn what was the matter.

'Most were drunk', we are told, 'to end the new bell wake.'

At Curdworth a new bell, inscribed 'Sancta Maria Virgo, intercede pro toto mundo' was presented to the church by a traveller who had lost his way in in the Forest of Arden and found the village by following the sound of a small bell. He vowed, we are told, to give a large bell which would be even more effective. One of the bells at Whitnash was taken down to be recast. On its way back to the church it was brought to a well between Whitnash and Radford – the source of Whitnash brook – to be re-consecrated. Perhaps it is surprising that such a place was chosen for the ritual, but a great many wells and springs which had been revered in pagan times were christianised and continued to be venerated. Unfortunately, the bell somehow fell into the well during the ceremony. It disappeared, and could not be recovered. But it was still able to toll, and when the country people wished to know the future they dropped stones into the well at night. The bell answered their questions eventually by ringing the following morning. One ring meant yes; two rings, no. The well no longer exists, but there is still a little stream, believed to possess healing powers.

Some churches had a problem with those who slept, not during the bell-ringing, but during the sermon. At St Peter's, Coventry, these people were roused by a whippy cane. The man who used it was the 'Penny Cane'. At Dunchurch sleepers were prodded with a fork-shaped piece of wood. The Church Beadle was often known as Robin Redbreast, from the red waistcoat that he wore as part of his uniform. In some churches he was equipped with a staff; it had a brass knob at one end and a fox's brush at the other. If working people were inattentive he used the brass knob; the aristocracy were given a tactful twitch with the brush.

Warwickshire churchyards have many unusual epitaphs. The most remarkable of all did not appear on the tomb for which it was intended. Shakespeare wrote it, we are told, for John Combe, who died in 1614. Combe made himself unpopular by lending money at what was considered to be the extortionate rate of ten per cent. His monument is still in Stratford Church, but without this inscription:

Ten in the hundred lies here engraved,
'Tis a hundred to ten his soul is not saved;
If any man ask who lies in this tomb,

> Oh! oh! quoth the devil 'tis my John-a-Combe.

Richard Davies, who died in 1639 at Brailes, is remembered with reverence:

> Though dead hee bee yet lives his fame,
> Like rose in June so smells his name.
> Rejoice we at his change, not faint,
> Death kild a man, but made a saint.

This was evidently a paragon among men. Elizabeth Mott paralleled him. She died in 1720, after 44 years of marriage and 42 children:

> A loving wife, a tender mother,
> Scarce left behind her such another.

Unfortunately, her tombstone is missing from the churchyard at Monk's Kirby, but the memorial to Thomas Lewis can still be seen. He died in 1849: after serving for 44 years as sexton.

> The graves around for many a year
> Were dug by him who slumbers here;
> Till worn with age he dropped his spade,
> And in this dust his bones are laid.

Another working man, a woodcutter who lived in the time of George III, has a plaque at Brinklow with a billhook, mittens, an axe, faggots of wood, and this verse:

> This man (his character to sum),
> From infancy was deaf and dumb,
> His understanding yet was clear,
> His heart was upright and sincere.
> He chiefly got his livelihood,
> By faggoting and felling wood:
> Till Death, the conqueror of all,
> Gave the feller himself a fall.

At Aston, John Dowler, a blacksmith who died in 1787, was commemorated:

My sledge and hammer lie reclined,
My bellows, too, have lost their wind
My fire's extinct, my forge decayed,
And in the dust my vice is laid;
My coal is spent, my iron gone,
My nails are drove, my work is done.

Some of these verses occur in different parts of the county, and are clearly traditional. The best known is perhaps one which appeared at Tysoe in 1798, though it could be found in many other places:

This life is a city of crooked streets,
Death is the market-place where all men meet.
If life were merchandise that money could buy
The rich would live and the poor would die.

Not unexpectedly, epitaphs often contained a moralising note. The fate of Lydia Eason of Stoke, near Coventry, was a clear warning to others: 'All who come my grave to see/Avoid damp beds and think on me', and here is a brass at Hampton-in-Arden:

Man, it behoves thee oft to have in minde
That thou dealest with the hand that shalt thou find:
Children bin sloathful, and wives bin unkind,
Executors bin covetous and keep all they find.

The dialect 'bin' for 'are' makes this particularly touching.

The present church at Great Wolford was built in 1833, but John Randal, who died in 1699, is buried in the churchyard, which is older. His epitaph runs:

Here old John Randal lies,
Who counting from this tale,
Lived three score years and ten,
Such vertue was in ale.
Ale was his meat,

Ale was his drink,
Ale did his heart revive,
And if he could have drunk his ale,
He still had been alive.

Not everyone was so tolerant of ale. Joseph Rowley, aged 27, was killed at Wolvey in 1853 at the Bull's Head, in a fight which broke out during the Harvest Home celebrations. The local parson composed what he considered to be an appropriate epitaph:

When Madness fires the young and gay
To dance Life's latest, shortest hour away;
Do thou consider well:
If this next step should prove my last,
Where shall I wake when Death my die has cast:
In Heaven? No! in Hell.

Rowley's friends were most charitable, and they scratched out the last three words.

A more tragic, violent death is commemorated at Sutton Coldfield:

As a Warning to Female Virtue,
And a humble Monument of Female Chastity,
This Stone marks the Grave
of
MARY ASHFORD.
Who, in the 20th year of her age,
Having incautiously repaired
To a scene of amusement,
Without proper protection,
Was brutally violated and murdered,
On the 27th May, 1817.

Mary Ashford was on her way home to Erdington from the High Street market in Birmingham, when she met a friend, Abraham Thornton, a young bricklayer from Castle Bromwich. He invited her to a village dance, and she danced with him all evening until they left, at 3 a.m. They walked to the house of a female friend of

Mary's in Erdington, and the girl went inside to change her dress. When she came out Thornton had disappeared. Mary went home alone; by now it was between 4 and 5 a.m. Two hours later her body was found in a water-filled pit at Sutton. She had been raped, beaten, and thrown in the pit to die. Apart from circumstantial evidence against Thornton, his shoes matched the foot prints at the spot. He was arrested and put on trial at Warwick Assizes. The evidence was complicated by differences of time on various clocks: apparently the standard time used in Birmingham was not followed in Sutton. Thornton was acquitted, and a storm of protest followed. The 'Mary Ashford tragedy' became a *cause célèbre*.

William Ashford, Mary's brother, decided to appeal against the acquittal by an ancient procedure called Wager of Battle. This would technically have allowed him the right to fight Thornton in single combat to determine his guilt or otherwise. Trial by battle was a legacy from feudal times. Such a combat took place outside the walls of Coventry at Gosford Green in 1398: Richard II intervened and stopped it. The Thornton trial was the last occasion in British judicial history when Wager by Battle was invoked. Thornton had to choose to prove his innocence by combat, which he did, and the case came before the Court of the King's Bench, at Westminster. William Ashford argued, through his lawyers, that Thornton had no right to wage battle in this case, since he was manifestly guilty. The court was then able to review the evidence of the lower court, and might have changed the verdict. However, in April 1818, the court declared itself unanimously of the opinion that Thornton was entitled to wage combat, since the presumption of guilt was not in fact so strong as to deprive him of his right. Ashford, being considerably younger and smaller than Thornton, was obliged to decline combat. The appeal was therefore stayed, and Thornton discharged.

Unfortunately for him, popular feeling was strongly against him, no doubt influenced by a number of ballads. He and his father, a builder from Castle Bromwich, were eventually forced to emigrate to America. Plays about Mary Ashford continued to be performed for at least fifty years. The identity of her murderer — if one accepts Thornton's innocence — was never discovered.

At least, so far as we know, Mary Ashford had the privilege of resting in peace in her grave. Others were less fortunate. At one time it was very difficult for doctors to obtain corpses for dissection, and this led to the practice of stealing newly-buried bodies from cemeteries. Even after the Anatomy Act of 1832 was passed to regulate the supply of cadavers to medical schools, the resurrection men continued to operate for about a decade. In Birmingham they were known as 'diggum uppers', and the most feared and notorious of the fraternity was Ben Crouch, who later served as a model for Charles Dickens' character, Jerry Cruncher, in *The Tale of Two Cities*. Stories of the 'diggum uppers' continued to circulate for many generations after their illicit trade ceased. 'About forty years ago', wrote Tom Langley in 1970, 'I was talking to a very old man who remembered as a child looking from an attic window in Icknield Street, Birmingham and watching lights in the Warstone Lane Church yard. His father told him, "the diggum uppers bin after Jobey Didlum". Jobey had been his playmate, recently dead. The medical school was in Edmund Street a few hundred yards distant.'

$$\multimap 4 \multimap$$

God send Sunday:
the World of Work

THE FARMING year officially began on Plough Monday, the first Monday after Twelfth Day, when ploughmen dragged a plough, decorated with ribbons, from door to door and took a collection. Later in the day the proceeds were spent on drinks. It is not surprising that this custom lasted in some villages into the 1930s. In some places there was also a procession of plough boys dressed in ragged but striking costumes to represent Molly, who carried a ladle, and the clown, with his horn. Then there was Bessy, whose hat-band explained:

> This is the man who carries the can
> And tots out good beer to every man.

At Ettington on Plough Monday the servant girls from the farms had to race from the kitchen door to the nearest furrow, pick up a clod of earth, and run back. This sounds easy, but they were chased by plough boys, armed with whips. If the girls could get back to their kitchens first and stick a feather in the clod of earth, the boys were obliged to forfeit their share of the plum pudding traditionally served at the Plough Monday meal.

Horses were vital to the farming economy. They were much prized, and purchased with great care. A traditional rhyme provided guidance for buying a horse:

> One white foot, buy a horse;
> Two white feet, try a horse;
> Three white feet, look well about him;
> Four white feet, go away without him.

Special words of command, now seldom heard, were understood by the horses. *An* meant 'move towards the left', and *eet*, 'move towards the right'; *comming gen* meant 'turn left', and *gee gen*, 'turn right'.

As soon as the state of the land permitted, bean setting began. At Shottery it traditionally started on St Valentine's Day and ended before the 21st of March. After bean setting the farmers provided a good meal of butcher's meat, a great rarity, and plum pudding. Cheese and cider were also sometimes supplied, for instance at Long Marston and Pebworth. Bean setting was followed by the planting of corn. At Long Marston before the first seed was set, the labourers whipped a cat in a barrel to death. Four seeds were set in each hole: 'One for the pigeon, one for the crow; one to perish and one to grow'.

John Purser, who was born at Ilmington in 1878, remembered the corn planting.

> Dibbers were used ... These were pear-shaped like a big, inverted pear, with a pointed steel cap to pierce the ground. Some were small, but where a large field was to be planted, an experienced man would use two long-handled dibbers, and walking backwards, would make the holes, two at a time, as he moved. Then came the women, with little calico bags tied round their waists, to drop in the corn. It was tiring work, done in wintry weather, for which they might get a shilling a day.

Like the beans, germinating seeds were protected by children stationed in the fields for long hours, armed with rattles or clappers. 'I was a youngster of nine when I began to earn money', wrote Joseph Arch, who was born at Barford in 1826. 'My first job was crow-scaring, and for this I received fourpence a day. This day was a twelve hours one, so it sometimes happened that I got more than was in the bargain, and that was a smart taste of the farmer's stick when he ran across me outside the field I had been set to watch'. Joseph Ashby of Tysoe, who was born in 1859, also started work as a bird-scarer at the age of nine. To cheer his loneliness 'he took to shouting so as to hear a human voice. This method had another convenience; you couldn't cry while you shouted.' Another possibility was to sing or chant rhymes like:

> Ye pigeons and crows, away! away!
> Why do you steal my master's tay? [tea]
> If he should come with his long gun,
> You must fly and I must run.

This came from Ilmington. Other villages had their own variants. Shottery, for example:

> Shoo-hoo, shoo-hoo!
> Away, birds, away,
> Tek a corn
> And leave a corn
> And come no more ter-day.

Villages long since buried under bricks and mortar possessed their songs. This is from Handsworth:

> Cooo-oo!
> I've got a pair of clappers,
> And I'll knock 'e down back'ards;
> I've got a great stone,
> And I'll break your backbone.

The beginning of the lambing season was announced by the shepherd, as soon as the first lamb appeared. He was rewarded with a large, thick pancake, which had been specially baked, and a cock was taken to the field, fastened to a peg by a piece of string, and everyone shot at it. Sheepshearing began on 1 June. From then on all the men and boys on the farm were fed in the farmhouse kitchen. Every man, even the blacksmith, was expected to take part in the shearing, which had to be completed while the moon was waxing. Afterwards came the sheep-shearing supper. Shakespeare has one in *The Winter's Tale,* and the clown has to buy provisions:

> Let me see: what am I to buy for our sheep-shearing feast? Three pound of sugar, five pound of currants, rice — what will this sister of mine do with rice? But my father hath made her mistress of the feast, and she lays it on. She hath made me four-and-twenty nosegays for the shearers, three-man-song men all, and very good ones . . . I must have saffron to colour the warden pies [pies made with warden pears]; mace; dates — none, that's out of my note; nutmegs, seven; a race or two of ginger, but that I may beg; four pounds of prunes, and as many of raisins o' th' sun [dried in the sun].

In more recent times the fare was less spicy, consisting of beef, stuffed chine, and beer, but in some places — Ilmington, for instance — posies of flowers were still laid on the men's plates. At Long Marston the sheep-shearing feast and the seed feast were held together. Beef, plum pudding, tobacco and beer were provided. These events continued in same form until perhaps the 1920s.

When the hay harvest came round each mower went out on the first day with a posy from his wife or sweetheart pinned to his smock. At Ilmington and Whitchurch a few stems of grass were left uncut at the end of the first swathe and twisted into the shape of a cock's head. When the rest of the field had been cut the mowers returned to the head and tried to sever it with their scythes, blindfolded. Each man who failed was fined a quart of beer, which was drunk by the company later. At Brailes a real cockerel was brought into the field, tethered by a string, and shot at. One one occasion the bird mysteriously survived until a man who suspected witchcraft loaded his gun with a silver sixpence.

Bringing home the corn harvest was the climax of the farming year. 'The farm labourers took pride in their work', says John Purser, and did not like change. In harvesting, the sickle gave place to the fagging hook and scythe. They in turn gave place to the mowing machine and reaper ... Mowing was a strenuous job, but some delighted in it. It needed skill rather than strength, though many men were not equal to it ... When time came for a break, one, Tom, used to say, 'Come on mates, let's go and sit with us legs uphill, and rest us backs'. They would sing:

> Some delight in hay-making,
> Some delight in mowing,
> But of all the jobs that I like best
> Give me a bit of turnip hoeing.

Under the old system of collecting tithes, which some elderly people remembered in the 1920s, the 'parson's men' went into the field after it had been cut and piled in 'shooks' or 'shucks' and took away one in every ten. Once the field had been emptied of its shucks, gleaning or leasing – the collection of stray stalks and ears – was permitted by custom, but only under certain conditions. If the farmer had not completely finished with a field he would leave a swathe uncut, one or two shucks uncollected, or put up a *bolten* of straw, as a signal that leasing might not yet begin. At Wellesbourne a horn was blown each morning and the names of the available fields were announced. At Ettington and Cubbington one of the church bells was rung every morning to tell gleaners that they might begin. At Tysoe the signal was given by the church clock striking eight. 'Until the first stroke of the bell ... no one of the company, woman or child, must pick an ear of corn from the stubble. This is the most strictly observed unwritten law ... a breach of which is punished by forms of lynching, which tax and do credit to female ingenuity.' Unfortunately, the writer does not specify. On the first day of gleaning, it was customary for the woman to wear a clean petticoat. Part of her first day's corn was made into a small stack and placed in the best bedroom; this would ensure a supply of food in the household for the coming year. People felt very deeply about the harvest. 'Though the disinherited had no great part of the fruits, still they shared in the achievement, the deep involvement and joy of it', wrote Mabel Ashby.

The last load was brought home from the fields with considerable ceremony. At Binton it was decorated with a T-shaped cross, at

Bishopton with leafy boughs, and at Wellesbourne with bright ribbons and flowers. The horses wore ribbons, rosettes and flowers. The driver, dressed in women's clothes, and the farm children in their best, rode on top. The labourers followed the cart, chanting and singing:

> Up! up! up! a merry harvest home.
> We have sowed, we have mowed,
> We have carried our last load.

Or:

> Hip! hip! hip! for the harvest home
> Now we've taken the last load home.
> I ripped my shirt and I teared my skin
> To get my master's harvest in.

When the last load reached the farm the mistress met the cart with cakes and ale. In the evening or a day or so later the Harvest Home feast took place. At Broad Marston it was held in a large barn, now demolished, known as the Shakespeare Barn. There is a tradition that Shakespeare often joined in the harvest fun there. He is said to have danced and sung on a flagstone in the floor of the Shoulder of Mutton in the same village.

An impressive Harvest Home procession 'at a village in the Vale of the Red Horse' took place in the 1890s. There were 'Flags and banners with harvest mottoes, the village drum and fife band, serving-men carrying sheaves of wheat and barley and beans, a gay waggon . . . laden with vegetables, a rustic bearing a huge loaf of bread upon a pole.' After touring the village the procession called at the house of the Lord of the Manor, Lord Willoughby de Broke, who gave bread and cheese to the farm servants.

Normally, the celebrations were less formal. The kitchen or a barn would be cleared for the farm people to have their meal. The food would be boiled beef and carrots, plum pudding and ale, and bread baked in the shape of an ear of wheat. After such a meal, 'My God', said an old countryman, 'you could crack a flay [flea] on my belly.' After supper labourers who had done wrong in some way during the harvest were punished. One of them was appointed judge, and the offender was 'laid on a bench and slapped on the breech with a pair of boots'. Shakespeare knew of this, too: 'Nay, give me not the boots', says a character in *The Two Gentlemen of Verona*. Occasionally there was violence; a man was killed in a brawl at Wolvey in 1853. But as a rule the celebrations ended peacefully with singing, including the health song;

> Here's a health unto our master, the founder of the feast,
> I hope to God in Heaven his soul may be at rest;
> That all things may prosper whate'ver he takes in hand,
> For we are all his servants, and all at his command,
> So drink, boys, drink, and see you do not spill,
> For if you do you shall drink two
> For it is our master's will.

Sam Bennett of Ilmington used to recite *The farmer's motto*:

> Let the wealthy and great
> Live in splendour and state,
> I envy them not,
> I declare it.
> I eat my own lamb,
> My own chicken and ham,
> I shear my own fleece
> And I wear it.
> I have lawns, I have bowers,
> I have fruit, I have flowers,
> The lark is my morning alarmer.
> So my jolly boys, now,
> God speed the plough;
> Long life and success to the farmer.

Other favourites were *Turmot Hoeing, The Leather Bottle, The Sprig of Thyme, The Jolly Herring,* and *All among the Barley.* There was also a mysterious bawdy song with a chorus of 'Ran de do dah day', which I have unfortunately failed to trace. The old-style harvest homes were becoming rare by the beginning of this century. Ragley, noted for its harvest feasts, held the last in 1908. By 1929 there was only one left.

The labouring man's pride in his work comes through in a song on the stocking of Bevington Waste, a little-known salient of Warwickshire, near Ragley. The Waste was a barren heath, but after four years' work in the early 1870s a gang of men turned over 400 acres to productive agriculture. One of the foremen, Arthur Allchurch of South Littleton, near Evesham, wrote a song which commemorates their work.

The wake of Bevington
Tune: *Auld lang syne*

Come all you jolly labouring men and listen to my song;
The theme is well known to you all, it is of Bevington.
Five years ago great oaks did grow 'mid thorns and briars long,
But now the labouring men have made cornfields of Bevington.

Chorus
For George and Dick and Fred, old Parker and his son,
And Arth and John and Alf and Tom, they all worked at
    Bevington.

Some folks did say, and well they may, it never would be done,
But when did brave hearts ever fail when backed by arms so
    strong?
So cheerily we went to work with spades and mattocks long,
Though many weary bones we brought from the work at
    Bevington.

When nearly done, then like a man, up Mr Webb did come;
Said he, 'I will stand treat, my men, when ere this job is done'.
He left a pound to buy some drink and didn't we have some fun,
And Boots and Booker had a fight at the Wake of Bevington.

And now the job is done and o'er, my song I now will end;
Heaven bless the fruits of this our toil and on us blessings send.
In years to come, passing this way, our earthly course near run,
We'll proudly say we mind the day we grubbed up Bevington.

When his 'earthly course' was nearly run, a labourer was sometimes obliged to take a job stonebreaking.

The job was a lonely one, on the grass verge of the road all the day. He must first break the stones down with his large hammer, and then use a small, blunt, double-headed one to finish them off. It was not as easy as it looked. He had to make sure of his mark, or he would make slow progress. Often, he would sit on part of this broken heap to get closer to the work, and so to ease his back. Occasionally he would get a passer-by to stop and talk. He would find a sheltered spot in the hedge for his midday meal of bread and cheese and a bottle of cold tea. When he started for home, it took him a while to find his road legs; and then he would hasten to his chimney corner and his warm meal. It was usually an old man who had to take such work. The pay was not as much as a labourer's, unless long practice had made him quick. It was paid for by the yard, and the stones must be of even size.

Another way out of labouring, only possible for a strong young man, was navvying. Children would call out:

> I'm a navvy, you'm a navvy,
> Working on the line;
> Five and twenty bob a week,
> And all the overtime.
> Roast beef, boiled beef,
> Puddings made of legs;
> Up jumps a navvy
> With a pair of sausage legs.

Sausage legs probably meant trousers tied round with string below the knee; and a bob was of course a shilling (5p).

There were many more trades in Warwickshire, and some are represented in St John's House Museum, Warwick. Goldfinches were called proud tailors – a term also used by Shakespeare – because it was thought that the souls of tailors, who used to sing at their work, had migrated into them. There were shearers, carders, spinners and weavers: the Throckmorton Coat, kept at Coughton Court, was completed in 1811 from sheep's back to finished coat in a single day, for a bet. There were smiths at nearby Alcester until they offended St Egwin. In their eagerness to make money, they began working seven days a week and when the Bishop of Worcester, who was later canonised, tried to dissuade them they

hammered loudly and sang to drown his voice. He cursed them and
their trade, and gave them all tails. The disgrace ruined them, and
the craft of smithing died out in the town.

Coal mining has existed in north Warwickshire for centuries, but
its customs and lore have received little attention. While they share
many terms and expressions with fellow miners elsewhere, others are
peculiar to their own county. The *basset* is the coal face. *Pufflers,
coddies* and *doggies* are miners in charge of various jobs. A *swilly* is a
short dip in the seam, and the *kelf* is the working space between
floor and roof. Some one *ringing it* is sitting down idling. *Let's coat
it* or *It's time to coat it* means that it's time to stop work. *Looseall*, the
first syllable pronounced *lowse*, is the signal for the end of the shift.
Miners leaving the pit probably met *the others:* a special term for
their white-faced comrades coming in on the new shift.
Warwickshire miners do not seem to have produced many songs,
but one was written as late as the 1960s by a miner in the now
closed Haunchwood Pit, near Nuneaton, entitled *The old miner*. A
brass in Baxterly Church commemorates two men lost in a fire at
the local pit on 1st May 1882, and nine others who died in a rescue
attempt.

At one time the Coventry weavers were better known, 'Tried
and true, like Coventry blue', originally referred to the blue dye in
Coventry ribbons. Joseph Gutterbridge, born in 1816, was
apprenticed to the trade of ribbon weaving in about 1830, and
discovered at least one custom 'against which my whole nature
revolted':

> Every newcomer was expected to pay for a gallon of ale, each of
> the other men in the factory adding a pint. The men would either
> strike or at any rate prevent the new hand from going on with his
> work until he had complied with this custom, so that it was
> morally impossible to resist. Sometimes the men would adjourn
> to a public-house to drink the beer, but oftener it would be
> brought into the shop. The older apprentices were allowed to
> share in these orgies, and the younger ones — lounging about —
> would get in an odd drink now and then.

This practice, usually known as a foot-ale, was widespread, and
applied not only to apprentices, but to any new workman.

Gutteridge refers disparagingly to the practical jokes played on apprentices, which were sometimes quite dangerous. Today, the jokes continue but they tend to be harmless. The new man is sent on a fool's errand for a left-handed screwdriver, a tin of elbow grease, a bubble for a spirit level, or some red oil for a rear lamp.

Initiation customs seem to be very much a part of any group with a coherent collective identity. At Kenilworth the choirboys put newcomers down a nettle-filled hole in the churchyard, known as the Monk's Hole, and watered them. In some Birmingham schools pupils still celebrate their departure for a job by hurling flour and eggs at each other, autographing shirts and blouses, garlanding their friends with toilet rolls, and ripping blazers and ties. This last led to court cases in 1972, when razor blades were used and caused injuries. The 'outcome' of the apprentice was his twenty-first birthday, which marked the expiration of his indentures, after a term of seven years. In Birmingham it was celebrated at the joint expense of the master, the apprentice, and the workmen. At twelve noon, guns were fired. This was the signal for work to stop and drinking and singing to begin. At one o'clock the ordinary dinner hour followed, and work continued from two until five. In the evening an outcome supper was held at a pub, where eating, drinking and dancing continued until midnight. The apprentice was lifted on to a table, and crowned with laurel or bays. Everyone crowded round, singing:

> Here's to him that's now set free,
> Who was once a prentice bound;
> And for his sake this holiday we make,
> So let his health go round,
> Go round, brave boys, until it comes to me,
> For the longer we sit here and drink
> The merrier we shall be.

In many ways this was a pre-industrial ceremony — it has similarities with the harvest homes — which survived into industrial times. So was Saint Monday, the practice of absenting oneself from work on Mondays. As late as 1864 a report on the Birmingham metal trades spoke of the loss of an 'enormous amount of time', not only by want of punctuality in coming to work in the morning and beginning again after meals, but still more by the general observance of 'Saint Monday', which is shown in the late attendance or entire absence of large numbers on that day. One employer has on Monday only about 40 or 50 out of 300 or 400, and the day is recognised by many masters as an hour shorter than others at each end.

Customs like this were a conscious or unconscious protest against the clock; in Birmingham, the noisy factory hooter was known as the 'bull'. 'How's the enemy?' meant 'What's the time?' Mrs Cecilia Costello learned this song in the factory where she worked in the 1890s:

> Oh, when you get up in the morning, don't forget to call,
> Kick the panels off the door and dislocate the wall;
> I must be there at seven o'clock the mortar for to mix,
> So don't forget to call me up at half-past six.

Rough music was sometimes played in the factory or workshop, a terrible noise produced by banging tools and materials. It might be to greet the outcoming apprentice or to annoy an unpopular foreman or blackleg.

Saint Monday was not always popular with the wives. It reduced income and coincided with wash day, known as execution day. In complementary street ballads, printed in Birmingham, the husband criticises washing day, and the wife responds with *Fuddling Day, or Saint Monday.* Here is a verse from each:

> The sky with clouds was overcast, the rain began to fall,
> My wife she beat the children and raised a pretty squall.
> She bade me with a frowning look to get out of the way;
> The devil a bit of comfort's there upon a washing day.
> *Chorus*
> For it's thump, thump, scold, scold, thump, thump away,
> The devil a bit of comfort's there upon a washing day.

> St Monday brings more ills about, for when the money's spent,
> The children's clothes go up the spout, which causes discontent;

And when at night he staggers home, he knows not what to say;
A fool is more a man than he upon a fuddling day.
Chorus
For it's drink, drink, smoke, smoke, drink, drink away,
There is no pleasure in the house upon a fuddling day.

In the country washing was done, not weekly, but fortnightly, and
the 'great buck wash' took place every ten weeks. The lye was
prepared from wood ash. The wash started on Thursday.
Everything was washed a second time on Friday or Saturday and
left to soak in the 'buck tub', the coarsest items at the bottom and
the finest on top. Monday saw the final rinse and hanging out. At
Stratford a piece of suet was added to the first washing. Any lye left
in the house was always thrown away on a Good Friday and no
washing was done on that day.

—⇒ 5 ⇐—

Sneeze on
Monday

'A FACE AS long as Livery Street': this Birmingham expression, still current, is very apt, if one knows the street in question. Allusions in other figures of speech unique to Warwickshire are not always so clear. Kitty Bitt, Berry's wife, and Bassen's miller have long been forgotten, though their names have lived on in these sayings: 'as big a fool as Kitty Bitt', 'just the thing like old Berry's wife', and 'like Bassen's miller, always behind'. To be 'like Hunt's dog' was to be undecided, for this dog would neither go to church nor stay at home. To 'think a lie, like Cox's pig' refers to an unfortunate animal who thought his breakfast was arriving when in fact the butcher was coming to kill him. Trotting Bessie is mentioned in the saying, 'all over aches and pains, like trotting Bessie'. No one knows who she was, but 'spotted and spangled, like Joe Danks's devil', refers to an itinerant showman. Some of these expressions are very striking: 'as sharp as Joel Hedge, who cut the bough from under him'.

Joel Hedge is echoed in, 'As clever as the man who built his leg in the chimney'. 'To jet like a crow in the gutter' means to strut.

'Neither my arse nor my elbow' means neither here nor there, and 'better than a bob in the eye with a broomstick', better than nothing. The self-explanatory 'rough as goss [gorse] chopped off the common' and 'dark as a black pig in a bean rick' are again typical of the vigorous expressions which ordinary people love to use.

A great deal of popular wisdom was handed down in this form. Life was often precarious, and luck, good health, and good crops, had to be carefully husbanded. It was unlucky to meet a white horse, without spitting at it. For a man to meet a squinting man was also unlucky, but a squinting woman was a sign of good luck. It was lucky to see the first lamb of the season facing you, but unlucky to see it tail first. Other lucky encounters were with a chimney sweep, provided that you spoke to him, a sailor, if you touched his collar, or a load of hay, when you needed to wish, and watch it out of sight. To see a piebald or skewbald horse was also a sign of good luck. A piebald horse, by the way, is a white one with black patches, and a skewbald is white with patches of any colour other than black. To see three magpies was lucky, but to see one, or any number flying from right to left was unlucky, unless you crossed yourself or removed your hat. The cuckoo was traditionally held to come to Warwickshire on 17 April. Heard on the left hand, he brought good luck; on the right, bad luck, throughout the year. You should also wish, on first hearing the cuckoo, or alternatively borrow two half-pence, for luck. The old half-penny piece went out of circulation some years ago, and I am not sure whether the belief has transferred to the new currency.

It was thought that the cuckoo changed into a sparrow-hawk during the winter, and there are many other beliefs about birds. For example, it was believed that the yellow-hammer drank three drops of the devil's blood each May morning. The crossbill was thought to have acquired his mis-shapen beak by trying to pull the nails out of Christ's hands as He hung on the cross. The wagtail was known as the gypsy bird: 'if you see a wagtail a gypsy won't be far away'. It was unlucky to kill an owl, and the cry of the screech owl was thought to be a warning of death. To make them be kind to the poor, children were often told this story, which Ophelia refers to in *Hamlet*:

Our Saviour went into a baker's shop where they were baking, and asked for some bread to eat. The mistress of the shop immediately put a piece of dough into the oven to bake for him. but was reprimanded by her daughter, who, insisting that the piece of dough was too large, reduced it to a very small size. The dough, however, immediately afterwards began to swell, and presently became of a most enormous size. Whereupon the baker's daughter cried out, 'Heugh heugh, heugh! – which owl-like noise probably induced our Saviour, for her wickedness, to transform her into that bird.

The pigeon – or almost any bird, for that matter – brought a warning of death if it dashed itself against the window of a house. It is also the most untidy nest-builder. It is said to have grown tired when the wren gave a lesson in nest-building, so it flew away, crying 'That'll do-o-o-o, that'll do-o-o-o'. People thought that if hair-cuttings were carried away by birds and built into a nest, as the nest rotted, the hair would fall from the head of the person to whom the clippings originally belonged. Apart from legends and beliefs about birds, there was a wide range of local Warwickshire names – buttermilk can (long-tailed tit), Jack squeaker (swift), thrice cock (missel-thrush), and Grecian (yellow hammer, so-called because of the markings on its eggs). Shakespeare used the local word for a heron when he wrote, 'I know not a hawk from a handsaw'. The robin and the wren were 'God almighty's cock and hen'. It was believed that

He that hurts a robin or a wren
Will never prosper on sea or land.

The robin's breast was said to have been scorched by hell-fire when it brought a beakful of water to give Christ on the cross.

Apart from his divinity, or perhaps because of it, the robin was a weather indicator. His song in the morning meant rain before night, but in the evening foretold a fine day on the morrow. The weather was of crucial importance to men living on the land, and they paid close attention to all the possible signs. Ilmington people believed that these things were signs of rain: black bats [beetles] running to the fireplace, black snails [slugs] facing east, the mist going from the mill to the hill. Others were indicated in rhyme:

When Ilmington hills begin to smoke,
Crimscot folks will wear their cloak.

If the cock crows when he goes to bed,
He gets up in the morn with a wet head.

When sheep do huddle by tree and bush,
Bad weather is coming with wind and slush.

If Friday and Sunday were wet, a wet week would follow. When the moon stood on its end, it meant rain, but if it lay on its back like a boat, there would be fair weather. Here is another Ilmington rhyme:

Wet on Good Friday and Easter Day
Means much good grass but little good hay.

The coming into leaf of the ash and the oak respectively sometimes provided contradictory weather omens. Two Warwickshire versions of the well-known rhyme tell us:

The oak before the ash, a summer of splash;
The ash before the oak, a summer of smoke.

If the oak's before the ash,
Then you'll only get a splash;
If the ash precedes the oak,
Then you may expect a soak.

A good crop of haws was a sign of a bad winter, since it meant that providence had ensured a supply of food for the birds. 'As the day lengthens the cold strengthens', was complemented by 'Never come Lent, never come winter'. Ilmington people said of the first two months of the year:

January dire
Freeze the pot upon the fire;
February fill-dyke,
And if it be white
'Tis the better to like.

> By Valentine's Day
> Every hen, duck and goose should lay.
> By David and Chad
> Every hen, duck and goose should lay, good or bad.

The end of the winter must have been a trying time for those who were old or infirm:

> March will search and April try,
> But May will tell if you live or die.

Other ominous sayings were: 'A warm May makes a fat churchyard', and

> When Easter falls on Lady-day's lap,
> Beware, old England, of a clap.

Of course, the weather governed work in the fields and gardens. Withies were cut when the leaves were the size of a mouse's ear, and elm leaves were a guide to planting barley and kidney beans:

> When the elmen leaf is as big as a mouse's ear,
> Then to sow barley never fear;
> When the elmen leaf is as big as an ox's eye,
> Then says I, 'Hie, boys! Hie!'
> When elm leaves are as big as a shilling,
> Plant kidney beans, if to plant 'em you're willing;
> When elm leaves are as big as a penny,
> You *must* plant kidney beans if you mean to have any.

Nothing should be planted when the moon is waning, and if pigs are killed, the bacon will shrink in boiling. But a waxing or full moon has a beneficial effect. The new moon should never be seen for the first time through glass. You must bow nine times to it, and turn over the money in your pocket. This will ensure good luck throughout the year, especially if you do it at each new moon. A wish made during the flight of a shooting star will come true, but whoever does this will regret it.

'A swarm of bees in July is not worth a butterfly,' says the

Warwickshire version of the well-known rhyme. At Ilmington it was believed that when a swarm left its hive the owner should assert his rights by 'ringing it', knocking on a fire shovel with a door key. If he neglected to do this he lost his rights to the swarm, but if he observed the custom he could follow wherever it went. There was another curious tradition connected with ownership at Hampton-in-Arden. A widow who re-married forfeited her estate unless she put her finger into a hole in a certain post and begged the consent of the lords of the manor.

Daily life in the home was filled with signs and omens. It was unlucky to pass the salt ('help to salt, help to sorrow') or to spill it. The ill luck of spilling it could, however, be averted by throwing a pinch of salt over one's shoulder into the face of the devil standing behind. It was unlucky to cross knives on the table, to kill a house cricket or money spider, to chop down a holly tree, to put anything other than a prayer book on top of a Bible, to go to a play on Friday, to pass someone on the stairs, to open an umbrella indoors, or to drink another's health in water. It was bad luck to say one's prayers at the foot of the bed, but lucky to fall downstairs. It was also lucky to pick up dropped gloves or an umbrella, or to find a horse-shoe. Egg shells should never be burnt, or the hens will stop laying. Similarly, if milk is put on the fire, the cows will go dry.

It was bad luck to throw out soap-suds on Good Friday because of the tradition that a woman threw dirty water over Christ as he was on his way to Calvary. It was considered lucky to eat pancakes on Shrove Tuesday, and grey peas and bacon on Ash Wednesday; this would ensure money in your pocket for the whole year. It is still considered lucky for every member of the family to stir the pudding at Christmas, and every mince pie eaten in a different house between Christmas Day and Twelfth Night brings a happy month in the coming year. It was bad luck to take holly into the house before Christmas Eve, or hawthorn, blackthorn and gorse at any time, perhaps because of their supposed connection with the Crown of Thorns. To prevent misfortune, the Christmas decorations were burnt on Candlemas Day (2 February); today this is done on Twelfth Night.

To mend an article of clothing while wearing it invited trouble, as did drying writing by the fire. If the palm of the right had itches, 'rub it on wood, it will come to good'. An itching right eye means

joy, a left eye, tears. For either eye to itch at night, however, is a
good sign. An itching nose means that you will be kissed, cursed, or
vexed — by a fool. Sneezing was thought to have particular
significance. To sneeze to the right was lucky and to the left, the
reverse. One sneeze meant wishing; two, kissing; and three, a
shocking bad cold, or alternatively, a disappointment. Four was a
letter; five, something better; and six 'is a journey you'll go'. The
day on which you sneezed was also significant:

> Sneeze on Monday, sneeze for danger,
> Sneeze on Tuesday, kiss a stranger,
> Sneeze on Wednesday, have a letter,
> Sneeze on Thursday, something better,
> Sneeze on Friday, sneeze for sorrow,
> Sneeze on Saturday, see your true love tomorrow.

Another version of the rhyme went on to say, 'If you sneeze on
Sunday you'll be a wicked person all the rest of the week'. Cutting
nails also had a meaning, depending again on the day of the week:

> Cut them on Monday, cut them for health,
> Cut them on Tuesday, cut them for wealth,
> Cut them on Wednesday, cut them for news,
> Cut them on Thursday for a new pair of shoes,
> Cut them on Friday, cut them for sorrow,
> Cut them on Saturday, see your sweetheart tomorrow,
> Cut them on Sunday cut them for evil,
> For all the week long will be with you the devil.

The last prognostication is reflected in another rhyme: 'Better a man
that's ne'er been born/Than pare his corns on a Sunday morn'.
Probably with the same aim of avoiding bad luck, teeth that came
out were salted and thrown into the fire.

The flowers of hawthorn and elder were unlucky in the house:

> Hawthorn bloom and elder flowers
> Will fill a house with evil powers.

However, the elder did have some good uses. Made up into a
toothpick it ensured protection from toothache, and a child wearing
a cross prepared from the white pith would never have whooping
cough. Whooping cough, or chincough, killed many babies, and

remedies were anxiously sought. In Birmingham infants were taken to Saltley gas works to smell the aroma; in other parts of north Warwickshire they were given a roasted mouse to swallow. At Pillerton the child was handed a piece of bread and butter every morning while the dew was on the grass, and a second piece was put out for the snails. The idea was that the illness would then be passed on to the snails. At Ilmington people thought a man on a skewbald horse would always suggest a infallible remedy. Riders of such horses must have been used to this and generally they suggested buttered ale. At Brailes three round slices of turnip covered in brown sugar were made into a sandwich. The liquor which drained off was given to the patient. Another cure was to grate three crow onion or crow garlic bulbs, wrap them in flannel, and put them in the patient's boots. Other varieties of wild garlic were also used. Another remedy was to pass the child three times beneath a 'moocher' — a bramble which has bent back to earth and re-rooted.

This recalls the practice of splitting the trunk of a tree in order to pass through it a weak, rickety or ruptured child. The tree was then bound or nailed together again, having absorbed the malady, or so it was thought. One such tree, an ash, stood on Shirley Heath by the side of the road leading from Hockley to Birmingham. It is depicted in an engraving published in the *Gentleman's Magazine* for October 1804. The writer says that:

Thomas Chillingworth, son of the owner of the adjoining farm, now about thirty-four years of age, was, when an infant of a year old, passed through a similar tree, now perfectly sound, which he preserves with so much care that he will not suffer a single branch to be touched — for it is believed the life of the patient depends on the life of the tree, and the moment that is cut down, be the patient ever so distant, the rupture returns, and a mortification ensues. It is not, however, uncommon for persons to survive for a time the felling of the tree. In one case the rupture suddenly returned, and mortification followed. These trees are left to close for themselves, or are closed with nails. The wood-cutters very frequently meet with the latter. One felled on Bunnan's farm was full of nails. This belief is so prevalent in this part of the county, that instances of trees that have been employed in the cure are very common.

There is a further account of one Thomas Rowe's being drawn through a tree in 1791 to effect a cure for rupture.

Almost as powerful a charm was believed to come from the touch of the hand of an executed murderer. As late as 1845 a murderer called Crowley was executed at Warwick, and a newspaper account said:

> At least five thousand persons of the lowest of the low were mustered on this occasion to witness the dying moments of the unhappy culprit. . . . As is usual in such cases (to their shame be it spoken) a number of females were present, and scarcely had the soul of the deceased taken its farewell flight from its earthly tabernacle, than the scaffold was crowded by members of the 'gentler sex' afflicted with wens in the neck, and white swellings in the knees, etc., upon whose afflictions the cold clammy hand of the sufferer was passed to and fro, for the benefit of the executioner.

In other words, women paid the executioner for what they thought was the curative touch of the dead man's hand. Another belief was that rheumatism might be cured by rubbing the affected part with the bone of a gibbeted murderer. Despite the fact that gibbeting was abolished in 1834, F. W. Bennett wrote that 'A great aunt of mine believed in this, and, until the day of her death in 1885 she kept in her work-box the finger bone of one – Palmer – who was gibbeted at the crossroads on the Stratford-on-Avon to Bidford road.'

Alternative treatment for rheumatism involved carrying the gall of a wild rose, wearing a string of corks tied round the leg below the knee, or allowing bees to sting the affected parts. Roasted mouse, as well as curing whooping cough, could stop bed-wetting in south Warwickshire. The brains of a freshly-caught hare were thought good for an ailing baby. A remedy for shingles was 'dowment', the black grease from church bells, though only dowment from the great bell would do. The liquid exuded from wheat heated on a shovel could also be used. These remedies were very common at one time. Croup and a sore throat could be treated by an emetic of goose oil, and in Shottery bead necklaces were worn as a preventive. Tobacco smoke blown in the ears was supposed to stop them aching. Infusions of tansy were given for colds, and dandelion flowers 'for the blood'.

Chilblains were rubbed with urine or with snow. Several cures for cramp came from Whichford. One was to carry a cork in the pocket, another was to draw the fingers between the toes – and then smell them. To carry a cramp bone taken from a leg of mutton was another possibility, but, if all else failed the sufferer's boots should be turned sole uppermost, presumably after he had removed them. Pins and needles called for the sign of the cross to be made on the top of the boot with a wet finger.

To return to infants' ailments, white mouth was treated, at least at Huncot and Wimpstone, by holding a young yellow frog by the hind legs and giving it to the baby to suck. Teething was made painless by giving the child a necklace to wear. At Stratford this was made of Traveller's Joy; at Whitchurch, of Halfwood; and at Southam, of nine strands of red sewing-silk. In 1915 there was an outbreak of scarlet fever at Whitchurch and a young mother told J. H. Bloom that she had removed the chance of infection by peeling some onions and burying the parings. People in Stratford hung an onion up in the house, and it was supposed to turn black if there was any infection present.

Warts should not be counted, otherwise they will increase in number. They might be removed by rubbing on nine successive days with the inside of a broad bean pod. An alternative was to apply black snails, which were then impaled on a blackthorn spike. As the snails shrivelled, the warts disappeared. If all else failed, a wart charmer might be consulted. John Day, who lived at Wimpstone in the 1880s, looked at the warts and made a nick in a piece of wood with a knife. Other charmers fastened a piece of meat to the warts; later it was removed and buried. As the meat decayed the warts disappeared. Sometimes charms were used, muttered so that the patient could not hear. The charmer expected a gift, preferably a lump of old iron, but never money or thanks. On the other hand, a charmer called Bennett, a carpenter by trade, did have a fixed scale of fees. In the early 1840s a mother took a boy who was suffering from whitemouth to him. He muttered a charm 'in such a manner that no word was intelligible', then took his fee.

A stye could be removed by stroking it nine times with a gold object, usually a wedding ring. At Halford they applied a cat's fur backwards, also nine times. In addition to all this treatment, there were various traditional sayings. Here is one from Ilmington:

> If you'd live to be old,
> Strip before you sweat
> And dress before you're cold.

It was important to eat well, when you could: 'better a belly bost [burst] than a good thing lost', ran the local saying. One delicacy in the part of the county adjacent to Staffordshire was groaty pudding, 'made of shins of beef, and groats [that is, dried oats, stripped of their husks], and after being well seasoned with salt and pepper, . . . baked in ovens'. Hogs' puddings were popular, too. They tended to burst during cooking, but this could be avoided by hanging an old clergyman's wig in the chimney. Apples gave one stomach ache if they were eaten before they had been christened; that is, before St Swithin's Day (15 July). Apples saved into winter were particularly useful:

> At Michaelmas and a little before,
> Away goes the apple along with the core;
> At Christmas and a little bit arter
> A crab in the hedge is worth looking arter.

So people said at Newbold.

Bread was baked by burning firing in the oven, removing it, and allowing the loaf to bake as the oven cooled. First, the oven was cleaned with a piece of wet sacking attached by a chain to a pole. This was called a 'malkin', a word also used in Warwickshire for a bedraggled woman. An infant was often put into the oven before the bread, to make sure that the heat was not too great. Each piece of dough was marked with the sign of the cross, to protect from witchcraft. If things went badly the bread might be sad, burnt or ropey [uneatable]. To guard against the last a piece of ropey bread was hung on the bacon cratch [rack] on Good Friday, and allowed to remain there for a year. It was thought that any loaf baked on Good Friday would remain fresh for a year, and many villages baked special loaves which were indeed kept for a year. Holes in the loaves were called coffins or cradles, depending on their shape. Small, hard lumps of dough were known as slut farthings or lazy backs – an indication that the kneading had not been done properly. A teaspoon of rain which had fallen on Ascension Day would, if added to the leaven, stop the bread from being too heavy. A newspaper reporter wrote in 1869: 'In a village a few miles north of Rugby, several old women might have been seen last Thursday [Ascension Day] busily engaged in catching the falling rain, which they carefully bottled for use during the ensuing year.' On the same day small cakes were baked at Warwick and Coventry, called God Cakes. Millers, whose flour was of course essential to the making of bread, were traditionally disliked as lecherous and dishonest. One miller, near Tysoe, gave as good as he got:

A stranger had remarked to him that all honest millers had a tuft of hair growing in the palm of the left hand. 'Ah', said the miller, 'and here you be', as he stretched forward his spread palm. The stranger was surprised, but managed a little bravery. 'You don't qualify, you see.' 'Hair be theer all right', said Styles, 'but it takes an honest man to see 'em.'

The other great staple was beer. At Ilmington four kinds were brewed: Black strap, Ruffle-me-cap, Fine and clear, and Table beer. At Alderminster Mrs Keyte made Double Ale, Single Ale, Very Good, Twine in the belly, Twice as many, Tip tap, Wuss than that, and Pin. She gave a labourer some Tip tap to drink and asked him why he laughed afterwards: 'Oi was wondering as 'ow you could brew two worse nor that.' Bad beer was said to be 'sour as varges' [crab-apples], and there was a children's beer called Tilly willy.

At Pillerton a quarter of malt brewed 100 gallons, 20 each of Strong ale, Table beer, Tit-me-tat, and Worse than that. Brewing was done mainly in March, with the last barley of one harvest, and October, with the first of the next. After brewing, a household would invite the neighbours who would come in with crusts of bread to dip in the new beer. This was called taking the shot. Till recent times Lord Willoughby de Broke preserved the old custom of keeping a large leathern jack filled twice a day with his October brew. It stood on the sideboard and callers could help themselves. Winter favourites were mulled ale, cider, or elder wine. These were spiced and heated in a cone-shaped muller or hooter, as it was called in Stratford. Each beverage was drunk in the proper vessel: beer, in a pewter tankard; stout, in a china mug; and cider, in a horn cup.

Perhaps it was an excess of good October which caused a

farmer's wife from Chacomb to have an accident. She set out for home from market, riding pillion to her husband. He was somewhat fuddled himself, and, when he got home, called to his son to come out and help his mother down. 'Where is she?' 'Behind, you fool.' 'Some way behind, for she ain't here.' Father and son got a lantern, and went in search. They found her in a ditch, where she had fallen. She had stanked up [dammed] the water, which was just beginning to trickle over her. 'Not a drop more tonight, thank you, maister,' she said, as the rescue party arrived.

—6—

Foul Fiend and Goblin Damned

MEON HILL, an outlying bastion of the Cotswolds, has been inhabited since Stone Age times. The story goes that it was created by the devil, who launched a great mass of earth through the air to overwhelm the newly-built abbey at Evesham. Fortunately, St Egwin was watching and praying. His prayers were so strong that they were able to stop the missile in flight, whereupon it fell to earth, and became Meon Hill. Between Alcester and Stratford there is a conical hill, called the Devil's Bag of Nuts. The devil was out gathering nuts – appropriately enough, on the Devil's Nutting Day (21st September). When he had collected a big bagful he had the misfortune to meet the Virgin Mary, who happened to be passing. The shock was so great that he threw down his bag of nuts before hurrying off, and they were turned into the hill. Anything dingy or dirty used to be called 'the colour of the devil's nutting bag' in Warwickshire. The devil is also remembered in the names for several common plants: Naughty Man's (or Cow) Parsley, Naughty Man's Plaything (Shepherd's Purse), and Devil's Nightcap (or

Hedge Parsley).

A Coventry musician, called Thomas Holt, who had nineteen children, sold himself to the devil to solve his financial problems. According to a pamphlet of 1642, *Fearefull Newes from Coventry*, when the contract expired the unfortunate man was found with his neck broken and his chest of gold turned to dust. More recently, a young man sold himself to the devil at Long Compton in the Close, a field with early earthworks near the church. He drew a circle in the centre of the field and read the Lord's Prayer backwards. When the devil appeared he had twelve imps as familiars and servants. Later, the man again raised the devil at Banbury Fair in the shape of a black cock. His fate has not been recorded.

> Have you seen the devil with his wood and iron shovel,
> Digging up potatoes in the turnpike road?
> Have you seen his wife with a broad-bladed knife,
> Scraping the potatoes in the turnpike road?
> Have you seen his daughter with a phial of dirty water,
> Washing the potatoes in the turnpike road?
> Have you seen his son with a double-barrelled gun,
> Shooting birds for dinner in the turnpike road?

These Warwickshire children's rhymes of the late nineteenth century imply at least a residual belief in the devil; they may owe their origin to the notion that on occasions the devil undertakes labour for mortals and gets through an enormous amount of work. And there was at least one labourer during that period who insisted on continuing to use a tinder box to make a light: the association between the devil and the brimstone in the new-fangled matches was too much for him.

There are not many stories about the devil in Warwickshire, but goblins and creatures of that kind were plentiful, as we can infer from place names. There is a Hob Lane at Sheldon and another at Yardley; a Hob's Hole at Barcheston, and another at Willington, together with a Little Hob's Hole. Tredington has a Great Hobbs' and Lower Hobbs' Meadow, and there is a Hobbin's Close at Great Alne and at Copt Heath. At Fillongley there is a Hobgoblin's Lane. Some places are particularly rich in such names. Northfield, in Birmingham, has Hob Acre, First Hob Ridge, Far Hob Ridge,

Hob Redding, Hob Croft, and also Jack Piece, Middle Jack Piece, Far Jack Piece and Cob's Field. Solihull has Hob's Moat, Hob Moor, Hoberdy's Lantern, Pucknell's Close, Jack Lands and Tib's Hall. Tib was one of Queen Mab's attendants. Shakespeare mentions Queen Mab under her traditional name in *Romeo and Juliet,* but calls her by a name of his own invention in *A Midsummer Night's Dream*: Titania.

Shakespeare was well aware of – and indeed may have shared – popular belief in these things. Fairy rings, 'orbs upon the green', are mentioned in the *Dream;* some Warwickshire people believed in them until within living memory. The expression 'played the Jack with us' is used in the *Tempest;* it was thought locally that Jack o' Lantern or Will o' the Wisp – like Puck – were mischief-makers. To be 'mabled' in Warwickshire once meant to be led astray by the Will o' the Wisp. Another malevolent creature was the Grim, which 'do like a skrich owl cry at sicke men's windows'. And again,

> When candles burne both blue and dim,
> Old folkes will say, 'Here's fairy Grim'.

Cobs and knops were hobgoblins, much feared. They were originally demon horses, and it is clear that belief in them remained strong in Warwickshire, for in parts of the county on All Souls' Day (2nd November) those brave enough went out carrying a simulated horse's head covered with a sheet to frighten the timid. The flibbertigibbet was a night demon who 'mopped and mowed' between the ringing of the curfew bell and the crowing of the first cock, with the object of terrifying young women. Not all the spirits were mischievous or malevolent. Dobbies were lazy creatures who would attach themselves to a particular farm. In times of trouble they sometimes exerted themselves on behalf of the family. Any unexplained noise was supposed to be caused by 'the ghost of old Flam' – apparently a harmless spectre, but no one seems to know who he was.

There was no shortage of ghosts in the county; nor is there, for this belief has remained very strong, right up to the present day. In 1974, Mr Colin Smith, a ghost hunter living near Birmingham, attributed the profusion of ghosts to the bloody history of the Midlands during the Civil War. Yet many apparitions seem to be modern. People living in a house at Short Heath, Birmingham, have heard a noisy ghost, thought to be female, banging about and leaving the smell of perfume behind her. Drivers on the Coventry-Rugby road have been terrified at the approach of a lorry on the wrong side of the road. At the last split-second, when a head-on collision seems inevitable, the lorry proves to be a phantom, and vanishes.

Another ghostly vehicle – this time a carriage and six – transported a Warwickshire worthy known as One-handed Boughton. The Boughton family lived at Lawford Hall, which stood not far from the Avon at Little Lawford, near Rugby. In Elizabethan times a member of the family lost an arm, and became known as One-handed Boughton. After his death his bed-chamber was haunted and his ghost was seen riding the countryside at night in a coach and six. A number of people tried to sleep in the bed chamber, but were driven out, terrified. In the time of Sir Edward Boughton, who held the title from 1722 until 1772, it was decided to lay the ghost. A team of twelve clergymen assembled, led by Parson Hall of Great Harborough. They proceeded, each with his bell, book, and candle, to the bedroom, to conjure the spirit into a bottle. Eleven candles went out, but the twelfth continued to burn, and Parson Hall duly stopped up the ghost in the bottle, which was thrown into a nearby marl-pit. However, the unsavoury reputation of the hall continued. The red hand, which came into the coat of arms when the family was ennobled, was thought to be a bad sign, and things were not improved by the murder of the head of the family, Sir Theodosius, by his brother-in-law, Captain Donellan, in 1780. Donellan was executed on a gallows near Wallace Street in Warwick, the following year. Four years later, the hall was pulled down, though there was considerable reluctance on the part of the workmen, because of their fear of the supernatural. Meanwhile, One-handed Boughton continued to ride, since part of the bargain when his spirit was conjured, was that he should be allowed two hours freedom every night. Early in the nineteenth century a bottle recovered from a pond near the site of the hall was thought to be the receptacle used by Parson Hall. Even this did not stop the ghost from pursuing its nocturnal rambles and calling upon late-night travellers to open gates until the late nineteenth century. There was another well-documented ghost a few miles away from Lawford, at

Barby. Unlike Parson Hall, the local clergyman did not attempt to exorcise it, but he left this account:

An old woman of the name of Webb, a native of the place, and above the usual height, died on March 3, 1851, at two a.m., aged sixty-seven. Late in life she had married a man of some means, who having pre-deceased her, left her this property, so that she was in good circumstances. Her chief and notorious characteristic, however, was excessive penuriousness, being remarkably miserly in her habits: and it is believed by many in the village that she thus shortened her days. Two of her neighbours, women of the names of Griffin and Holding, nursed her during her last illness, and her nephew, Mr Hart, a farmer in the village, supplied her temporal needs; in whose favour she had made a will, by which she bequeathed to him all her possessions.

About a month after the funeral Mrs Holding, who, with her uncle, lived next door to the house of the deceased (which had been entirely shut up since the funeral), was alarmed and astonished at hearing loud and heavy thumps against the partition wall, especially against the door of a cupboard in the room wall, though all the furniture had been removed, and the house was empty. These were chiefly heard about two o'clock in the morning.

Early in the month of April a family of the name of Accleton, much needing a residence, took the deceased woman's house, the only one in the village vacant, and bringing their goods and chattels, proceeded to inhabit it. The husband was often absent, but he and his wife occupied the room in which Mrs Webb had died, while their daughter, a girl of about ten years of age, slept in a small bed in the corner. Violent noises in the night were heard about two o'clock, thumps, tramps, and tremendous crashes, as if all the furniture had been collected together, and then violently banged on the floor. One night at two a.m., the parents were suddenly awakened by the violent screams of the child, 'Mother, mother there's a tall woman standing by my bed, a-shaking her head at me!' The parents could see nothing, so they did their best to quiet, and compose the child. At four o'clock they were again awakened by the child's screams, for she had seen the woman again; in fact she appeared to her no less than seven times, on seven subsequent nights.

Mrs Accleton, during her husband's absence, having engaged her mother to sleep with her one night, was suddenly aroused at the same hour of two by a strange and unusual light in her room. Looking up she saw quite plainly the spirit of Mrs Webb, which moved towards her with a gentle appealing manner, as though it would have said, 'Speak, speak!'

This spectre appeared likewise to a Mrs Radbourne, a Mrs Griffiths, and a Mrs Holding. They assert that luminous balls of light hovered about the room during the presence of the spirit, and that streams of light seemed to go up towards a trap-door in the ceiling, which led to the roof of the cottage. Each person who saw it testified likewise to hearing a low, unearthly, moaning noise — 'strange and unnatural-like', but somewhat similar in character to the moans of the woman in her death-agonies.

The subject was, of course, discussed; and Mrs Accleton suggested that its appearance might not impossibly be connected with the existence of money hoarded up in the roof, an idea which may have arisen from the miserly habits of the dead women. This hint having been given to and taken by her nephew, Mr Hart, the farmer, he proceeded to the house, and with Mrs Accleton's personal help made a search. The loft above was totally dark, but by the aid of a candle there was discovered, firstly, a bundle of writings, old deeds, as they turned out to be, and afterwards a large bag of gold and banknotes ... But the knockings, moanings, strange noises, and other disturbances did not cease after this discovery. They did cease however, when Mr Hart, having found that certain debts were owing by her, carefully and scrupulously paid them.

An Ilmington man with a pack of harriers became obsessed with hunting to the exclusion of everything else, including attendance at church. One night he went out to his hounds when they were howling, but they did not recognise him, and tore him to pieces. Ever since, his ghost has gone hunting on Christmas Eve and New Year's Day. If he sees anyone and gives a casual command, say, to open a gate, it must not be obeyed, or the person will fall into his power and be carried off for ever. There is more than a hint in this story of the baleful Wild Hunt which rode at nights, taking up unwary individuals, and sometimes giving warning of impending disaster. To return to Ilmington, the village seems to have been particularly well populated with ghosts. Pig Lane was haunted by a coach with headless horses and driver, carrying the ghost of a local magnate who had murdered a neighbour. The spectre of Edmund Golding, a parish clerk who died in 1793, used to be seen in the church at nights, walking up and down and muttering responses.

Other travelling apparitions were the ghosts of highwaymen. Swirling mists across a lonely stretch of Watling Street near Nuneaton have long suggested a phantom horse and rider, believed to be the ghost of Dick Turpin on its way to search for gold in the lost village of Stretton-Baskerville. It was more usual, perhaps, for ghosts of highwaymen to frequent the site of their execution. A spot by the Chester Road in Birmingham where a highwayman was gibbeted is said to be haunted, as is Sutton Park, where Tom King, another of the same fraternity, was burned to death. Certainly, violent death often gave rise to ghost stories. On Blacklow Hill, near Warwick, dismal bells are thought to be echoes of the bells on the horse which carried to execution Piers Gaveston, the favourite of Edward II, in 1312. At Guy's Cliffe there is a ghostly lady and a band of armed men, who are believed to be part of the same execution procession. At Chesford Bridge, on the Leamington to Kenilworth road, the ghostly figure of a woman could be the spirit either of a murderer or her victim. A servant at nearby Dial House Farm killed her mistress in 1820, and was hanged at Warwick before a crowd of 10,000 people. The Blue Lias Inn at Stockton, near Rugby, which was a farm-house in the eighteenth century, is haunted by the ghost of a red-haired farm labourer, killed by his master who found him in bed with his wife on returning from market. The situation of the farmer's wife in bed with a labourer has the ring of truth, and is confirmed by ballads. The vengeful killing, however, was fortunately not common.

At the White Swan Inn, Harborne, Birmingham, a presence manifests itself as a cold draught, a tap on the shoulder, or the sound of footsteps. This is thought to be the ghost of John Wentworth, a man of property who was secretly courting a poor girl. He provided a coach to bring her to meet him at the Swan in a private room. One day there was a mishap and she was thrown out of the coach and fatally injured. She died in that same room, and there John

Wentworth, after going mad with grief, shot, first his dog, and then himself. Another suicide haunts Dick's Garret at Aston Hall, where a man hanged himself because of 'the pangs of despised love'. Tantalisingly, there are no further details. Astley Castle, near Stockingford, is haunted by the ghost of Lady Jane Grey. It was one of the homes of her father, the Duke of Suffolk.

Haseley Pool at Charlecote is haunted by the ghost of Sir Thomas Lucy, whose body was thrown into the pool in 1262. He was murdered by his servants, but we do not know for what reason. The learned Fulke Greville, whose ghost is said to haunt Warwick Castle, was stabbed to death by a disgruntled manservant. Clopton House at Stratford has several ghosts. One is that of Margaret Clopton, who drowned herself in 1563 because her father refused to consent to her marriage. It is said that Shakespeare had her in mind, when depicting Ophelia. Another is the spirit of Charlotte Clopton, who died during an outbreak of the plague in 1564. She was quickly buried in the family vault at Stratford, in the parish church. A week or so later there was another death in the family, and the tomb was re-opened. The coffin was found to be open, and Charlotte's body was discovered upright, leaning against the wall. She had been prematurely buried, and in her agony had bitten into her own shoulder. Her ghost subsequently haunted Clopton House, and provided Edgar Allan Poe with the basis of one of his tales, *The fall of the House of Usher*. Finally, the unhappy house is also haunted by the ghost of a priest who was murdered there, in the sixteenth century. The body was dragged along the landing into a bedroom, and a thin, dark stain which runs along the floor is said to be an indelible bloodstain.

Not all ghosts are easily identifiable. At Hillborough a lady in white and a stag appear in a field, which was enough to prevent people from passing through the place after dark. Alscot has the nightmare figure of a being, half calf, half man. At Ragley Park a mysterious white lady sits on a stile at midnight and drinks out of the brook. A black man's ghost also haunts the park. He is said to have been unjustly killed in a duel by a white man. Popham Seymour, who owned the hall at the time, died after a duel in 1699, but both he and his opponent were white.

Within living memory a black dog, seen running down a hill at Lower Quinton, turned into a woman. Charles Walton, a ploughboy at Alveston, met a dog on the way home on nine successive evenings. On the final occasion a headless lady in a silk gown rushed past him, and the following day he heard of his sister's death. Another black dog with a matted, shaggy coat and green eyes roams in Whitmore Park at night. People avoid the area, since to see the dog means a death in the family. During the second World War at Brook House, Snitterfield, which used to be the Bell Brook Inn, a big black dog was seen. It ran over the tilled earth of the garden without leaving footprints. In addition, the people living in the house once saw 'a large oval ectoplasm' appear and 'hover round for an hour' in the former bar parlour. No explanation has ever been offered.

Fenny Compton is the scene of the appearance, from time to time, of a ghostly light, a blue and yellow ray, which floats over the range of hills between the village and Burton Dassett. In 1923/4 it was seen moving about in the churchyard. Mickleton, near Meon Hill, has a ghost identifiable by the booming noise it makes, and known as the Mickleton Hooter. The noise is said to be made by a ghostly cow, which some people have identified with the Dun Cow, the once benevolent creature which became distracted and had to be killed by Guy of Warwick.

Fillongley Church is said to be haunted by monks; noises are heard, and cowled figures have been seen in the Lady Chapel. The altar stone here was brought from Maxstoke Priory at the dissolution, and the monks are presumed to have followed. On the narrow path leading to the church people sometimes have the feeling of being forced back by unseen hands.

In 1820 a farmer returning home from Southam market was murdered. The next morning a man called on the farmer's wife and described how her husband's ghost had appeared to him on the previous night. The ghost displayed stab wounds on its body, named the murderer, and indicated the place (a marl pit) where the corpse was concealed. A search was made, the story found to be true, and the alleged murderer committed to Warwick Gaol. At the trial, Lord Chief Justice Raymond ruled that the evidence of a ghost was inadmissible; in any case, it had not appeared to give evidence. The crier was then ordered to summon the ghost, which he did, three times. On the non-appearance of the ghost the judge acquitted the prisoner and ordered the accuser to be detained. This man later confessed to the crime, and was executed after the following assizes. That any credence should have been given to his evidence indicates a strong local belief in the supernatural. Belief in ghosts still persists in Warwickshire.

'I was going home from here [a pub] and gooin' across the fields there was a traction engine standing in the corner by the gate. Well! just as I got agen it, all at once the fly wheel started to goo round like mad and I knowed it were a ghost a-driving it 'cos there was no steam in the boiler.' This was reported by F. W. Bennett, in the 1930s, but there was still great interest in ghosts in 1974, judging from reports in the *Stratford Herald*. A barmaid at the Salford Hall Hotel, near Bidford, felt a tap on her shoulder, and turned round to find the room empty. The presence she felt normally confines itself to Room 5, where, said the managing director somewhat inhospitably, 'many visitors ... have had their sleep disturbed. There was the poor chap who woke up suddenly in the night and thought that someone was sitting on his bed. The coat of arms over the bed was glowing mysteriously. An Irish girl couldn't sleep at all because of the strange atmosphere which she felt in the room.' The tragic background to the story is that a nun was found dead in this room on the very night when her sister was stabbed to death in Buckinghamshire.

Walton Hall Hotel in Stratford has more than one ghost. Several people claim to have seen a spectral white horse which gallops over the front lawns at five yearly intervals, on 9 October. The ghost of a youth has also been seen, in the cocktail bar, in the library, and in room 117. 'A waiter', says the newspaper account,

felt a cold blast, looked up and saw a white figure. A receptionist just 'felt convinced that she was not alone', she just couldn't stay in the room a second longer, although there was nothing to see.

The proprietor's daughter-in-law, Mrs Leslie Fields, hung all her husband's clothes away in Room 117. She returned to find them strewn across the floor. Her young children also described how they had played with a strange man who suddenly appeared in that room. After careful investigation it was confirmed that there had been no human visitors that night. A golden retriever, Josh, flatly refused to go past the room door.

The traditional explanation is that one of the ladies of the house was having an affair with a prince. Her husband returned unexpectedly and found them together. Presumably while the prince was trying to get away, the husband shot not him, but, either by design or by accident, his horse. Soon afterwards the lady gave birth to a boy, who was mentally subnormal. He had to be shut in the house, by means of bars which can still be seen at some of the windows in the west wing. He died in childhood. I have found no trace of this story in print, before the newspaper article, yet in 1929 J. H. Bloom wrote that 'Ghost stories are not very common in the neighbourhood of Stratford-upon-Avon'.

— 7 —

Churn, Butter,
Churn

SELLY OAK in Birmingham is said to be a corruption of Sarah's Oak, from the name of a witch hanged from it. A variation of the story is that she was hanged for witchcraft and buried there, the oak springing from the stake which was driven through her heart. Writing of charms and illnesses thought to be caused by witchcraft, J. A. Langford said: 'These superstitions exist in our large towns as well as in country villages – among the mechanics as well as the peasantry of the county.' This was in 1875, and he went on to describe how tricksters took advantage of such credulity. Among the 'many such cases from the police reports of our own enlightened town [Birmingham]' he quoted the case brought before the magistrates of Ann Archer, who was charged with obtaining fourpence each from Ann Lovesay and Sarah Hyde 'under the pretence of telling their fortune'. This was Ann Lovesay's evidence:

> I went to the prisoner's house, and told her that I was a married woman, and did not want to hear any love affairs, but wished to

learn whether I should ever come into possession of some property that I expected. Hyde, who is a young woman, went with me to have her fortune told also; and she was told that there was a dark young man in love with her. There was a fair-haired woman and a dark-haired woman, it was said, who would be the cause of great strife between them. We asked the prisoner what she charged, and she said 4d. She also said that she would have to tell my fortune by the globe (produced, and which was a piece of plain glass resembling in shape a large egg), as the cards were no use for me. She looked into the globe, and said that she could see in it the two gentlemen who would receive my property. I did not look into the globe myself, but I suppose that I should have seen nothing in it if I had. There were ten people in the prisoner's house waiting to have their fortunes told.

A mild confidence trick of this sort seems insignificant compared with the violence which suspected witchcraft provoked in the south of the county. We again owe the details to court appearances. John Davis of Stratford came before the Warwick Winter Assizes in 1867 on a charge of wounding Jane Ward. The details are worth quoting at length.

The prisoner, with his family, up to the time of his arrest, had resided in Sheep-street, Stratford-upon-Avon, and they had laboured under an impression that the prosecutrix, who occupied an adjoining house, had bewitched them. In spite of efforts of friends to the contrary, they persisted in the delusion, and frequently narrated, with singular circumstantiality, visits which had been paid them in the night time by spirits. Some of these, they stated, entered the dwelling by descending the chimney, and when they landed in the room they went through a variety of capers such as seizing the furniture, and pitching it about the apartment, pulling the clothes off the bed, and even tossing the inmates up into the air. One young girl, who was an invalid, and was obliged to recline upon the sofa, solemnly declared that a man and a woman came down the chimney on one occasion, both being headless, and taking her by the body, cast her violently upon the ground, then tossed her up into the air, and performed similar feats with the sofa. The statement created so great a stir in the town that the police were called in to investigate the matter, and although they pointed to the accumulated dust around the feet of the sofa in proof that no such thing could have happened the prisoner and his family declared their firm belief that witches had been there, and the only way to break the spell was to draw blood from the body of the prosecutrix, who was suspected of having bewitched them. A day or two after, the prisoner rushed into the house occupied by Jane Ward the complainant, and inflicted a frightful gash in her cheek. He inflicted a wound half an inch in width and two and a half inches deep. When he saw the blood flowing down her face, he exclaimed, 'There, you old witch, I can do anything with you now.' At the station, he said, in answer to the charge, 'Serve her right: she can do no more for me now. I have drawn first blood.'

Even more tragic consequences attended another case a few years later. Ann Tennant, an old woman of eighty, was murdered with a pitchfork at Long Compton in 1875 by a labourer named Haywood whose defence was that 'he had been bewitched [by the woman] and prevented from working properly by witches' spells, and that there were sixteen others in the village that deserved similar treatment'. He alleged at his trial that the water supplied to him contained witches. He believed that the evil eye of the old woman was responsible for the sickness and death of cattle and horses, and indeed for almost any misfortune which happened to the villagers. 'From statements made at the inquest', commented the *Warwickshire Advertiser*, 'it seems that these absurd beliefs are shared by others in these parts.' As a further proof of the justice of his case, the accused asked the court that the body of the victim should be weighed against the church Bible, an old test for a witch. He was ordered to be detained during Her Majesty's pleasure, and died a few months later in Warwick Gaol. If the law and the press were sceptical about witchcraft, the people at neighbouring Brailes evidently were not, for in the same year they went to Tysoe in a body, sought out a woman whom they suspected, and scored her hand with a corking pin. Drawing a witch's blood in order to get the better of her was known to Shakespeare:

> Blood will I draw on thee, thou art a witch,
> And straightway give thy soul to him thou serv'st.
>
> (*Henry VI*, Part I)

Long Compton was noted for its witches, even before this case; it was said that there were enough of them to draw a load of hay up Long Compton Hill. Their reputation perhaps owes something to the village's proximity to the Rollright Stones. The stone circle is just over the border in Oxfordshire, but some of the monoliths including the King Stone, are in Warwickshire. The origin of the stones is said to be this. When Rollo, the Dane, was about to invade England, he was told by a wise man that

> When Long Compton you shall see,
> You shall King of England be.

Rollo marched victoriously until, on the way towards Long Compton, calling on stick, stock, and stone, he approached the top of the ridge which looks down on the village. Before he could catch sight of Long Compton, he was confronted by a witch, who stopped him in his tracks by saying:

> As Long Compton thou canst not see
> King of England thou shalt not be.
> Rise up stick, and stand thou stone,
> For King of England thou shalt be none.
> Thou and they men hoar stones shall be,
> And I myself an eldern tree.

The king was turned into what is now called the King Stone, a group of his knights became the stones known as the Whispering Knights, and the rest of his army formed the great stone circle of Rollright. It is said, to this day, that they bleed if pierced by a knife. Another local tradition says that the stones can never be counted; yet another that no gate on the way to the stones will stay shut. There is a story that a farmer called Humphrey Boffin 'fetched the King Stone down to his court-yard to cover up a water course. It took eight horses to draw it there and even then the traces broke. He thought it safer, after this, to put it back. It only required one horse to drag it back up the hill'. Witches' sabbaths are thought to have taken place at the stone circle, and if the village girls ran naked round the circle at midnight on Midsummer's Eve, they might see the image of the man they were to marry.

The witch who turned Rollo to stone was clearly both powerful and patriotic. Her colleagues were often more limited both in effectiveness and in outlook. There was one, however, who told George Bailey of Wimpstone that she could bring his sister to him from a distance of twelve miles, and did so by taking twelve new pins and putting them in an apple which she threw into the fire. after muttering a charm. In 1914 it was said that Nance A. of Brailes could suspend girls from the ceiling by the hair, or make them walk on the ceiling like flies. She could appear herself in the guise of a white rabbit. She would sometimes bake for neighbours, but, if offended, would put a spell on the oven door so that it would not open. Sarah Brookes, of Rookery Cottages, Knowle, was reputed to be able to change into a black cat. One night someone threw a fork at this cat, cutting its leg. Ever afterwards Sarah had her arm in a sling. Mrs F. of Long Compton could assume any form – mouse, cat, rabbit – so long as it was white. One night while in the guise of a rabbit she was run over, and her arm was bandaged the next day. Betty L., of Tredington, was similarly wounded while in the shape of a cat. Next day, she had a wound in her right hand, which never healed. For some reason, she developed a grudge against a local farmer, who then found that he could not get his fire to light, his beer to brew, his butter to come, or even his cow to go down the lane to be milked. The spell was only removed when he gave Betty a weekly present of milk. All these cases occurred early this century.

Writing in the 1930s, F. W. Bennett recalled:

Less than twenty years ago I knew an old woman who had quite a local reputation for being a witch. . . . Her prophecies as to the precise date and hour of a sick person's death came gruesomely true. There is no question that she greatly presumed upon her eerie reputation in order to get round the village *mumping*, as she called it, which . . . means that she used to call round on the people and collect from them oddments, a bit of tea from one and a few scraps of bread from another.

Bennett's witch apparently did not have to resort to sanctions like some of her colleagues. Betty H. of Darscot could prevent the fire from burning, make the cheese fail, or stop the butter from coming. She assumed the form of a hare at times, was once wounded by gunshot while doing so, and had a bad leg for the rest of her life.

Spells which adversely affected the work and production of the farm could be disastrous. Country people had a number of defences and safeguards. To prevent milk being bewitched during churning it was possible to insert a red hot poker, throw in a silver coin — since witches hated silver — or say this rhyme:

> Churn, milk, churn,
> Come, butter, come;
> The great bull of Banbury
> Sha'n't have none.

The rhyme came from a lady, born in 1850, whose mother used it at Ettington. Another method of removing a spell from cream was to pass a dead man's hand widdershins three times round the churn. Alternatively, dead men's hands being no doubt in short supply, a sprig of rowan might be used. It was unlucky for anyone to go into the dairy while butter was being made, but the bad luck would be averted if the intruder helped with the churning.

Again at Long Compton, Mary W. put one Henry Jeffs under 'an ill tongue', but was forced to remove the spell when the local schoolmaster — somewhat inexplicably — burned some of his own finger- and toe-nail parings in the oven. Similar stories come from Brailes and Tysoe; they recall the reference in the *Comedy of Errors*: 'Some devils ask but the parings of one's nails, a bush of hair, a drop of blood'. At Willington in the 1880s a servant lifted a spell on the cows by taking a cow's heart, sticking it with pins, and roasting it in the oven, so that the witch should be drawn there. A small animal, the like of which none of them had ever seen, came and 'scratted' at the door, trying to reach the heart. The creature died, and the spell was broken. The servant's grandson told the story to J. H. Bloom.

Billy Balson, who was immortalised in the saying, 'Billy Balson'll 'ave yer', lived at Wolvey. He had the power both to foretell the future and to bewitch. He could locate stolen money, and blight crops. When he was on his death-bed people heard the sound of horses galloping up to the door; presumably the devil's conveyance was arriving to collect his own. Within living memory, Mrs H. of Long Compton was seriously ill, but could not die in the presence of her relatives and neighbours, so they left the room. Hearing a commotion they went back to find the room in disorder, the old lady dead, and a pigeon flying out of the window.

Betty P., another witch, who lived between Tredington and Honington, haunted the wall of the church after her death: people would see her there, smoking her pipe. It is said that Compton Wynyates graveyard contains the tombstone of the witch, Jane Story, and the stone watcher on Caesar's Tower at Warwick Castle indicates the spot, according to tradition, where Moll Bloxham jumped to her death. She was allowed to trade in the tower, selling the castle's surplus milk and butter for her own profit. The privilege was removed, however, after the townspeople had protested to the earl about her high prices. Moll then sought supernatural aid and disappeared; whether by design or accident is not recorded. She was replaced by a large black dog which began to roam the castle. Three clergymen summoned to exorcise it drove the creature to the top of Caesar's Tower, and it leapt into the river below. Its spirit, or that of Moll Bloxham, still lies imprisoned below the weir.

It was believed in Warwickshire that witches sometimes buried a sheaf of wheat below the window of one whom they wished to destroy. As the sheaf rotted, the person's body withered. In 'about 1910' Mary Dormer Harris was told by a Mrs Bennett of Charlecote 'that horse-shoes drove away witches. Before her time the witches used to meet in the far Park. One old witch called Diana rode a buck. ... Witches in these parts were very active. They could turn into cattle. It was necessary to draw their blood in order to prevent them hurting you. ... They occasionally 'strike' people. Thus a man with his cart going 'uppards' [to Kineton or Ettington] found that he and his horses couldn't go on.' An obelisk at Umberslade, which was in fact erected in 1745 to enhance the view on the skyline, is still said to mark the meeting place of the last coven of witches to meet in Warwickshire. In 1945 on St Valentine's Day, the body of Charles Walton, a seventy-four year-old hedge-cutter, was found under an oak tree on the slopes of Meon Hill. It was pinned to the ground with a pitchfork, and had the sign of the cross slashed on the throat. An investigation by Fabian of the Yard produced nothing. Local rumour had it that

Walton had mysteriously communicated with birds and animals and had the power of the evil eye. Perhaps his ritual murder was to break or forestall a spell.

— 8 —

Marriage, Birth and Death

THE SOLEMN moments in life were surrounded by a host of omens and ceremonies, large and small. The coming of a wedding might be foretold simply by the girl's cheek burning, or alternatively by the appearance of three magpies: 'One for sorrow, two for mirth, three for wedding, and four for a birth.' If the girl were curious as to who the man thus indicated would be, she scattered fern seed in a garden or wood at midnight on Midsummer's Eve, saying:

> Fern seed I sow, fern seed I hoe,
> In hopes my true love will come after me and mow.

She would then see the young man's image.

Once the wedding was arranged, the future bride seems to have been particularly vulnerable to misfortune. She had to avoid putting on her ring before the ceremony, though she might try on her clothes, so long as she avoided wearing her complete wedding costume at the same time. She might not mark her trousseau with her new name before the wedding, or it would never happen. To 'change the name and not the letter' was to 'change for worse and not for better'. The winter months were not propitious: 'Who marries between the sickle and the scythe [from after harvest till the coming of spring] will never thrive'.

On the wedding day itself, precautions redoubled. The bride must not look in the mirror, either before she started to dress, or after she had finished. The colour of her dress was important:

Married in white, you have chosen all right;
Married in green, ashamed to be seen;
Married in grey, you will go far away;
Married in red, you will wish yourself dead;
Married in blue, love ever true;
Married in yellow, you're ashamed of your fellow;
Married in black, you will wish yourself back;
Married in pink, of you he'll aye think.

Not surprisingly, blue was popular, this being the colour of heaven, as well as of true love. The guests would wear 'bride-laces' of blue ribbon tied to their left arms, and sprigs of rosemary and broom. One last stitch must be added to the bride's dress before she set out, and she must not look back at her old home. Little of this care in preparation is taken today, but a belief still widely held is that it is unlucky for the bride to see the groom on her wedding day before they meet at the church.

On the way to the ceremony it was unlucky to meet a funeral, and a sign of certain death if one of the undertaker's black horses should turn its head towards the bridal carriage. On the other hand, it was fortunate to meet a grey horse; consequently, greys were normally used for bridal carriages. The church path would be strewn with flowers and rushes, and one of the bridesmaids would walk before the procession carrying the cake – made by the bride herself, to demonstrate that she could cook. In the church the cake would be broken, handed round, and eaten. The bride would carefully retain a piece, thus ensuring that the groom remained faithful. At the christening of the first child it might be eaten, since the baby would become a new pledge of fidelity. The bridesmaids, too, kept a piece of cake. Passed through a wedding ring and laid under their pillows, it would give them dreams of their future husbands. A bride cup was also circulated in church and, later, a two-handed loving cup would be passed round the village. This was perhaps the last vestige of the old 'bride ale' custom which was enacted by the local people for Queen Elizabeth at Kenilworth castle in 1575. First the bride groom came in with sixteen companions, followed by morris dancers. Then followed three women, each carrying a spice cake, and a young lad with the brides-cup. Behind him were two elderly men leading the bride, then twelve bridesmaids. When all were assembled the young men entertained the party with the sport of quintain.

The ring was of great importance, and would be ritually cleansed of evil by a sprinkling of holy water. It was very unlucky to lose it afterwards, especially since it was used as a charm against infants' complaints. In default of a proper wedding ring, a curtain ring might be used ('marriage by curtain ring' signified a hasty wedding), and even the church key could be used as a substitute.

There was a belief that if a bride appeared for her wedding dressed only in a smock, her husband would not be liable for any debts which she had previously contracted. A lady in Birmingham must have been particularly anxious to avoid such earlier obligations, for she appeared at the altar naked, having undressed in the vestry. This was in 1797.

Rice would be thrown at the couple as they emerged, together with the occasional old slipper. In earlier times it was grains of wheat, standing for fruitfulness. Today, confetti is thrown, and not only at church weddings. The main Registry Office in Birmingham does a brisk trade on Saturday mornings, and the area is deep in confetti afterwards. Sunshine was a good sign, as Adam Bede knew:

> Happy is the bride the sun shines on,
> Blessed is the corpse the rain rains on.

At the wedding feast, if an older sister of the bride was unmarried, she was forced as a mark of her disgrace to dance in her socks, or in the pig trough. After the feast the couple went to their new home, where the first to enter 'would be the one to clean the boots'. The bride would bring with her a handful of cinders from her mother's

house, which would be used to help kindle a fire in her new home.
Once kindled, it should never be allowed to go out.

'A good year for nuts is a good year for babies': another piece of
Warwickshire wisdom. Like marriage, birth was surrounded by a
host of potentially evil influences. A pregnant woman had to avoid
the house of any one thought to have the evil eye, or buy off such a
person with small gifts. Alternatively the evil influence could be
countered by carrying something made of silver, such as a coin. A
hare crossing the path of the mother-to-be could cause her child to
be born with a hare lip, but this could be avoided if the woman
stopped and made three rents in her shift.

At the birth itself the room would be crowded with people, in
order to guard against changelings. Immediately after birth the
child's mouth would be rubbed with a mixture of butter, sugar and
honey — 'the treacle of heaven' — to give sweetness to his tongue. It
was lucky for him to be born with his face partly covered by the
caul, which would then be called a mask. Even a caul which was not
a mask was useful, for it could be burnt as a means of divination: the
number of 'bosts' [bursting noises] it gave would indicate the
number of children the mother would bear from then on. A mask
was especially valuable, as it safeguarded its possessor from
drowning. It was therefore particularly sought after by sailors. At
Stratford it was believed that the child would go abroad if the mask
were lost. At Birmingham a dried caul carried on the person was
thought to prevent rheumatism.

There was a belief that a child born with hair on his arms and
hands was born to be rich. If he arrived on Christmas Day he would
have the power to see spirits. The day of the week was also
significant. In Warwickshire the well-known rhyme, 'Sunday's
child', ended:

> Thursday's child is inclined to thieving,
> Friday's child is free in giving,
> Saturday's child works hard for his living.

It was unlucky for the baby to go down before going up, and the
helpers would if necessary get up on a chair with him before taking
him downstairs. It was also unlucky for the child to see himself in a
pool or mirror immediately after birth. If snow were on the ground,

the baby might be rolled naked in it — this was done at Ilmington — in order to make it strong. At Stratford, only its feet would be rubbed in the snow, to bring immunity from chilblains.

It was normal for the mother to have four days' seclusion in the bedroom after giving birth. During this time she had special nourishment, known as 'caudle', a mixture of old ale, oatmeal, sugar and spices. It was the duty of the wife of the local squire, if there was one, to provide the caudle, which the new father would go and collect from her kitchen. If no old ale were available, water from certain wells, termed 'caudle wells', might be used. Crimscot, Shottery, Snitterfield, Long Compton and Cherrington — and no doubt other places — all had caudle wells. If, despite being fed by its mother, the new-born baby seemed restless, and made continual sucking movements with its lips, it was thought to be needing something which the mother could not provide. Hare's brains, pounded into a jelly, would be prescribed, and it was again traditional to approach the wife of the local squire to supply the hare.

If the life of the new-born baby was in danger the ceremony of baptism would be performed by the midwife, though children so treated were said to be only 'half-baptised'. If they died, they would be buried on the north side of the church, with the unbaptised and the suicides. For the proper ceremony in church, the baby would be robed in a white garment, called a 'chrisom'. If the parents were too poor to buy one, they might borrow the communal chrisom belonging to the village, which was kept by the priest. The mother would return it when she went to be churched; it was thought wrong for her to go out on ordinary business before this. At the baptism salt was placed on the baby's tongue, with the exhortation: 'Receive the salt of wisdom, that God may be gracious to thee'.

The godparents, of whom there were never more than three, were sometimes still given the old name of 'gossips'. It was an evil portent if the child did *not* cry during the ceremony of baptism. A common christening gift was a silver apostle spoon, which it was very unlucky to lose in later life. Another useful gift was a piece of coral. It had the double benefit of helping to form the baby's teeth and to protect it from witchcraft. The first teeth had to be treated with some care when they came out. They were sprinkled with salt as a general remedy against being used for ill. If a dog ate one, the child's new tooth would be a dog's tooth. It was a good thing for a milk tooth to be put in a mouse's hole so as to ensure that the new tooth would be as small as a mouse's. The children in at least one Warwickshire family still put a tooth that has come out under the pillows the following night. The fairies, in the shape of the parents, then remove it and leave sixpence. With inflation, the sixpence has recently become 5p.

It was considered unlucky to weigh a baby or to cut its nails before it was twelve months old. The nails should be bitten, not cut, to shorten them, otherwise the child would turn out to be light-fingered. High infant mortality and low medical care caused people to rely heavily on charms. Convulsions in infants were prevented by a red ribbon sewn round the baby's neck (Whitchurch), a ninefold ply of red silk, knotted in front and fastened on immediately after birth (Stratford), or a loop of twisted stems of Travellers' Joy (also Stratford). A shrub of the nightshade family, called Half Wood, was used for the same purpose at Charlecote and Whitchurch. 'The stems were cut into half-inch lengths, threaded through one end, so that each section hung suspended'.

In a close community, everyone knew how well or otherwise married couples got on together. A merciless children's rhyme might well apply to some:

> Heeper, peeper, chimney sweeper,
> Had a wife and couldn't keep her;
> Had another, didn't love her,
> Heeper, peeper, out goes she.

Popular feeling despised any household where the man was not the master:

> If the sage tree thrives and grows,
> The master's not master, and that he knows.

A wife might progress from taking charge to beating her husband; there are misericords in the parish church at Stratford which show a wife beating her husband, who is upside down and also being bitten by a dog; another woman, holding a man by his beard, whacks him with a saucepan.

A husband who allowed himself to be henpecked (or worse) was usually thought to have only himself to blame. But a woman beaten by her husband might be completely defenceless, so the community tried to help her by showing its contempt – chaff might be heaped on the doorstep as a sign of reproof. No doubt this hint of public disapproval often caused a husband to control his temper. But not always: in the seventeenth century John Chambers of Tanworth-in-Arden was hanged for the murder of his wife, as we know from a ballad preserved by Samuel Pepys. Its full title is: 'The bloody-minded husband, or the cruelty of John Chambers, who lately lived at Tanworth, in Warwickshire and conspired the death of his wife, hiring a servant to shoot her with a musket, which he accordingly did; for which they were both arraigned, found guilty, and executed for the same.'

Adultery was strongly disapproved of, and local feeling towards the offender was expressed by playing rough music, or 'lewbelling', as it was called in parts of Warwickshire. A case which occurred at Brailes in 1909 was reported in *The Illustrated London News*:

PUNISHMENT BY EFFIGY: A LEWBELLING BAND AND THE
DUMMIES OF AN ERRING PAIR

Lewbelling is a custom which, although it has almost died out, is occasionally observed, and such an observation took place recently. The word 'lewbelling' seems to be derived from 'lewd' and 'belling', roaring or bellowing. A 'lewbelling' occurs when the morals of a married man or a married woman have left something to be desired, and neighbours wish to show their disapproval. In the case illustrated, the effigy of the man was made first, and exposed for three days: the effigy of the woman was exposed for two days. The figures were placed side by side, the woman's arm upon her lover's shoulder. A band of thirty and more youths and boys, beating all kinds of utensils, paraded the village for three nights. On the third night, after dark, the effigies were taken down and burnt. The dummies were set up opposite the woman's house. The fear of this form of public exposure is said to act as a great deterrent.

An old inhabitant of Charlecote remembered a similar ceremony. 'Young men and lads armed themselves with tin cans, etc., and went to both offenders' houses three nights in succession, and marched into three parishes, – Hampton Lucy, Charlecote, and Wasperton. On the third night they burned the man's and woman's effigies in front of both their houses at Hampton Lucy. The last time it was done in this district was in 1892.' J. H. Bloom recalls a further instance from Whatcote, for which he unfortunately gives no date: 'a coarsely dramatic representation of the offence [of adultery] was made at stated intervals on the route, stones were hurled through the window's of the offender's house, and the effigies, which were exceedingly gross, were burnt before his windows.' Faced with such strong disapproval, those who had offended popular opinion often felt obliged to move elsewhere.

When deep and mutually recognised incompatibility between married people occurred as, inevitably, it did from time to time, a form of unofficial divorce was sometimes practised. This was wife-selling – not the haphazard and degrading business which has often been assumed – but the transfer with due public ceremony of a wife to a pre-selected new partner. The Warwickshire children's rhyme perhaps echoes the practice:

> Nebuchadnezzar, the King of the Jews,
> Sold his wife for a pair of shoes;
> When the shoes began to wear, good lack,
> Nebuchadnezzar wished her back.

Traditional procedure was carefully followed. In village and small town markets the woman might appear, led by a halter through three turnpike gates or three villages, paying toll like any other commodity. She might be sold for one, two or three half-crowns. Many such sales took place with no record other than local memory. But in the bigger towns they were occasionally mentioned in the press. In August 1773 the *Annual Register* noted:

> Samuel Whitehouse of the parish of Willenhall, in the county of Stafford, sold his wife, Mary Whitehouse, in open market, to Thomas Griffiths, of Birmingham. Value, one guinea. To take her with all her faults. (Signed) Samuel Whitehouse. Mary Whitehouse. Voucher: T. Buckley, Birmingham.

The complete openness of the proceedings shows the participants really believed they were taking part in a legal ceremony. Wife sales must have been frequent, judging by the following statement printed in *Aris's Birmingham Gazette* of March 1790: 'As instances of the sales of wives have of late frequently occurred among the lower classes of people who consider such sales lawful, we think it right to inform that, by a determination of the courts of law in a former reign, they were declared illegal and void, and considered (a light in which religion must view them) as mere pretence to sanction the crime of adultery'. Undeterred, 'the lower classes of people' continued to follow the custom. At least one further sale was recorded at Smithfield Market, Birmingham, in 1834. Even after 1857, when divorce became legal for the first time, proceedings were so expensive that they were in practice still not available to ordinary people, and the old sales of wives continued. Apparently, women did not exercise a similar right to sell their husbands. No case of this has been recorded in Warwickshire, but in 1852 one husband was leased to a woman other than his wife. The details came to light when the man was charged with assaulting his wife, and fined 2s 6d [12½p]. In his defence he produced a written contract, drawn up by a lawyer:

> Memorandum of agreement made and entered into this second day of October, in the year of our Lord 1852, between William Charles Capas, of Charles-Henry Street, in the borough of Birmingham, in the county of Warwick, carpenter, of the one part, and Emily Hickson, of Hurst Street, Birmingham aforesaid, spinster, of the other part. Whereas the aforesaid William Charles Capas and Emily Hickson have mutually agreed with each other to live and reside together, and to mutually assist in supporting and maintaining each other during the remainder of their lives, and also to sign the agreement hereinafter contained to that effect ... And for the true and faithful performance of this agreement, each of the said parties bindeth himself and herself unto the other finally by this agreement, as witness the hands of the said parties, this day and year first written above.

It is difficult to be quite sure whether this was a form of confidence trick by Capas to persuade Emily Hickson to live with him despite his previous marriage, or whether they were both convinced that this was the proper form. Certainly, Mrs Capas, when giving evidence in the assault case, stated, apparently as a matter of course, that her husband was not living with her, 'but was "leased" to another female'.

One much-married Ilmington man had three wives, though not simultaneously, and successively outlived all three. Two of them he remembered with gratitude, but not the third:

> God bless Pitchitee-Patch,
> Likewise Save-all;
> And the Devil take Tear-all.

There were a vast number of signs and portents of death. The cry of the screech owl, a toad crossing one's path, birds — and especially pigeons — flying against the window, dreams of losing a tooth — all these were signs of death. Even so common a thing as the howl of a dog or a clock stopping could be a sign. Rather more unusual portents were a mouse on the bed, the fall of a flitch of bacon from its hook, the accidental ringing of a bell, or a clock striking thirteen. Square-shaped creases accidentally formed in a tablecloth were known as coffins, and an imperfection in a candle which made the tallow curl or wind was a winding sheet: both were obvious warnings.

The transplanting of parsley — which presumably should have been propagated only by seed — meant a death in the family who owned the garden within a year. Another ill omen in gardening was to cut through a white bryony root, which, near Stratford at least, was called a mandrake root. There is a record of an old man digging near Stratford in 1908 who was unfortunate enough to do this. He stopped work, became greatly worried and concerned, and within the week, fell down some steps and broke his neck: a remarkable example of the power of self-suggestion. A spade, or any workman's tool, was unlucky, if carried into the house at the end of the day on their shoulders: 'If in your house a man shoulders a spade/For you or your kinsfolk a grave is made.' Similarly: 'If you buy a broom in May/You're sure to sweep a corpse away.'

When anyone was dying, it was thought that the feathers of a game bird in a pillow, especially pigeon feathers, would cause

prolonged suffering. This is why it was always removed. When the
death had occurred there was a whole series of small duties to be
performed. The bees were told of their master's death, but first their
attention was attracted by knocking on each hive with a key.
Otherwise, at best they would not thrive, at worst they would leave
their hives. The well-being of the bees and of the household seem to
have been closely linked. 'If your bees fall sick and die/One of your
house will soon in churchyard lie.'

Clocks were supposed to stop at the moment of a death. Every
lock in the house was then unfastened. It was important to avoid
looking into the mirror in the room where the corpse was lying;
otherwise the reflection of the dead person would appear in it.
Before the funeral, the mirrors were shrouded. If the hand of the
corpse remained damp and clammy, it was a sign of another death
coming in the family. An alternative belief was that if the flesh
remained soft, another death would follow, but not if it were stiff.

If the prepared grave were left open on a Sunday there would be
another death within a month. At Napton it was supposed that a
corpse lying over Sunday — it should have been buried by Saturday
— would take two more with it. A man took two women, and a
woman, two men. The corpse remained in the house until the
funeral, when it was carried through the front entrance, feet first.
The door was left open until the return of the mourners, otherwise
another death would follow. 'The procession of mourners was very
orderly, the eldest or nearest relatives following first, and then two
by two [in descending order] to the youngest or more distant
relatives and friends, all carefully dressed in black. This was
borrowed if they had none and were too poor to buy, as it was
unthinkable not to wear some black clothing as a mark of respect.' If
one of the black horses pulling the hearse turned its head towards a
door and neighed, when the cortege was passing it was believed that
there would be a death in the house within a year.

If the corpse was carried over private ground it was supposed
that a right of way had been created. Such routes wre known as
church ways or corpse ways. There is one over Brailes Hill, by
which the dead of Brailes were said to have been carried to Bredon.
The paths from Stratford to Wilmcote, and from Whitchurch to
Binton, are other examples. Shottery Road at Stratford was known
to old people as 'Berrin Road' since it was used for the passage of

funerals.

Some families possessed a winding sheet which served as a pall.
One used for many generations at Whichford was made of
hand-woven linen, and had strips of lace which formed a cross when
the sheet was folded. The church bells rang a muffled peal for an
important person or a former bell-ringer. For others, there was a
short tolling or telling of one bell to attract attention, followed by
three clear strokes for a child, six for a woman, and nine for a man.
The saying, 'Nine tailors make a man' is probably a corruption of
'Nine tellers make a man'. Finally, there was a stroke at intervals of
a minute for every year of the dead person's life.

On the Sunday morning after the death of a relative, female
mourners attending church remained seated and veiled during the
singing of hymns. The graves of the dead were decorated with
flowers, not only on the anniversary of their death, but also of their
birth. Shakespeare's rosemary 'for remembrance' was used at both
weddings and funerals.

The Hobby Horse Forgot:
Popular Sport and Pastimes

ROBERT DUDLEY, Earl of Leicester, entertained Queen Elizabeth at Kenilworth Castle in 1575. The festivities lasted from 9 to 27 July, and we are fortunate in having an eye-witness account of at least part of the proceedings, from Robert Laneham. Some commentators have deduced from passages in *A Midsummer Night's Dream* that Shakespeare was there, too.

The entertainment was provided mainly by local people, who presented their usual sports and amusements. Captain Cox, the ballad singer from Coventry, was there, and some of his fellow-townsmen performed their Hocktide play for the queen. More of a spectacular pageant than a play, it re-enacted the defeat and massacre of invading Danes, on Hock Tuesday in 1002. At the end the enemy survivors were led away captive by English women, 'whereat her Majesty laught and rewarded the performers with two bucks and five marks in money'.

The Coventry people seem to have enjoyed watching drama. The Grey Friars, part of whose church still remains, were celebrated for their performance of the Corpus Christi cycle, named after the day on which it was given. The subject was announced in a prologue by the Vexillator, who carried a flag with the subject painted on it. Large crowds flocked into the city to see the performances, which continued until the sixteenth century. Some of the texts have survived, including the famous Coventry carol. After the bombing of the Cathedral in 1940 it was sung at one of the first services held in the ruins, as a re-affirmation of indestructible values.

At Henley a fifteenth-century guild performed miracle plays and processions. Its guild hall still stands, on the north side of St John's Church. Folk plays were performed at different times of the year in many towns and villages. The traditional date at Kenilworth was 5 November, and performances continued within living memory, but Christmas seems to have been the most popular time elsewhere.

Behind the curious rhetoric and knockabout comedy is a deep seriousness and solemnity, for the plays concern the eternal truths of life, death, and rebirth. This version is from Newbold, near Rugby:

Characters: Father Christmas, St George, Turkish Knight, Dr Brown, Moll Finney, Humpty Jack, Beelzebub, Big Head and Little Wits.

The actors huddle together in a group and as the turn comes of each he steps forward and so enters.

FATHER CHRISTMAS:

I open the door, I enter in
I see bold face before I win.
Whether I sit, stand or fall,
I'll do my duty to please you all.
In comes I, old Father Christmas,
Christmas, Christmas or not,
I hope old Father Christmas
Will never be forgot.
A room, a room, a gallant room,
A room to let us in.
We are not the ragged sort.
Old activity, new activity,
That never has been known,
The dreadfullest battle on earth was seen
In this room shall be shown.

If you don't believe these words I say,
Step in, St George, and clear the way.

Enter St George, flourishing his sword.
ST GEORGE:
In comes I, St George, St George,
The boy of courage bold.
With my broad sword and spear
I won ten pounds of gold.
I slew the fiery dragon
I drove him to the slaughter
And by these means I won
The King of Egypt's daughter.
And if any man dare step within this room
I'll hack him up as small as dust
And send him to Jamaica
To be made into mincepie crust.

Enter Turkish Knight.
TURKISH KNIGHT:
In comes I, a Turkish knight,
In Turkey land I learnt to fight.
I'll battle with thee, St George
And if thy blood is hot
I'll quickly set it cold again.

ST GEORGE:
Tut, tut, thou little fellow
Thy talk is very bold
Just like those little Turks
As I've been told
If thou be a Turkish knight
Pull out thy sword and fight
Or pull out thy purse and pay
I'll have satisfaction before I go.

TURKISH KNIGHT:
There's no satisfaction about it.
My head is made of iron
My body's lined with steel
Therefore I'll battle with thee St George

To see which on the grave shall fall.

They fight. Turkish Knight falls. Father Christmas approaches, and draws out a bottle:

FATHER CHRISTMAS:
Fear not, I have a little bottle by my side
It is hocum slocum aliquid spam
I touch the crown of this man's tongue
And the crown of his head
Will drive the heat through his body
And he will rise again.

Turkish Knight kneels before St George:
St George, St George, pardon me, pardon me
For I'll ever be thy slave.

ST GEORGE:
What, pardon a Turkish knight?
Never. Arise once more and try thy might.

They fight. Turkish Knight falls, supported by Father Christmas. Enter Moll Finney.

MOLL FINNEY:
St George, St George, what has thou done?
Thou hast surely ruined thyself
By killing my only son
Is there a doctor to be found
To cure this man lies bleeding on the ground?

Enter Doctor.
DOCTOR:
In comes I, the doctor Brown,
Cleverest doctor in the town.
O yes there is a doctor to be found
To cure this man lying on the ground.

MOLL FINNEY:
What's your fee?

DOCTOR:
Ten guineas is my fee
But five I will take of thee.

MOLL FINNEY:
Thank 'ee doctor. What can you cure?

DOCTOR:
Hipsey, pipsey, palsy, gout,
Pains within and pains without
Bring me an old man that has been
In his grave threescore years and ten
With a broken tooth, I'll pull it out
And put it back again.

MOLL FINNEY:
If it's true, thou art a clever doctor.

DOCTOR:
Clever? D'ye think I'm like these quack doctors
Go walking up and down the streets?
They tell more lies in five minutes
Than I do in seven years.
I have a little bottle by my side
In it galvanic drops
I twist the root of this man's tongue
And the crown of his head
I'll drive the heat through his body
And he will rise again.

ST GEORGE:
Arise, arise, thou curly Turkish knight
Go back to thine own land and tell
What old England has done for thee
Tell 'em we will fight
Forty thousand men like thee.

Enter Humpty Jack.
HUMPTY JACK:
In comes I, old Humpty Jack
Wife and family on my back
Some at the workhouse, some at the rack
I'll bring the rest when I come back
Roast beef, plum pudding
Old ale and mince pie
Who likes it better than old Father Christmas and I?

FATHER CHRISTMAS:
Aha, ha. A mug of your Christmas ale, sir,
Will make us merry and sing
But money in our pockets
Is much a better thing.
Now ladies and gentlemen
Give us at your ease
Give Christmas pies
Or what you please.

Enter Beelzebub.
BEELZEBUB:
Here comes I, Beelzebub,
On my shoulder I carry a club
In my hand a dripping pan
Please to give us all you can.

Enter Big Head.
BIG HEAD:
In comes I, Big Head and Little Wits,
My head's so big and my wit's so small,
I'll sing a song to please you all.

Sings:
There was an old man came over the sea,
A ha, but I won't have him;
Came over the sea to marry me,
And his old grey noddle, his old grey noddle,
His old grey noddle kept shaking.

My mother she told me to open the door;
I opened the door and he fell on the floor.

My mother she told me to get him a chair;
I got him a chair and he sat like a bear.

My mother she told me to make him some toast;
I made him some toast and he ate like a ghost.

My mother she told me to make him some cake;
I made him some cake and it made his tooth ache.

My mother she told me to take him to church;

I took him to church and he fell off his perch.

My mother she told me to take him to bed;
I took him to bed, next morn he was dead.

This play was performed every year at Christmastide at Newbold until the end of the nineteenth century.

There was an old man came over the sea

Further diversions for Queen Elizabeth at Kenilworth including hunting and bear-baiting. The bear-baiting took place inside the castle. The bandogs (mastiffs) were tied up in the outer court, and 'thirteen bears' were chained to posts in the inner court. Then the dogs were released and there was a fierce battle. These blood-thirsty sports were popular in Elizabethan times, and for several centuries after.

Morris dancing performed 'according to the ancient manner' by 'six daunsers, Mawd Marion, and the fool' was always popular with Warwickshire men and continued in unbroken tradition within living memory. At Ilmington it was in decline by the end of the nineteenth century. But in about 1906 a villager named Sam Bennett learned the tunes from the old pipe and tabor man, and the steps from former members of the side. Three years later Cecil Sharp collected the dances from him. The Ilmington morris side has gone, but the dances are still performed in the county, often by Birmingham sides. Sam Bennett died in 1951, aged 85, and a fiddle and bow are carved on his headstone in the little churchyard. Ilmington men are said to have danced at the old Cotswold Games.

A Warwickshire man, Robert Dover, the eccentric lawyer from Burton-on-the-Heath, either founded or revived an annual festival or sport held on a hill – now Dover's Hill – where the counties of Warwickshire, Worcestershire, Gloucestershire, and Oxfordshire meet. With some interruptions his 'Olimpick Games' continued from 1610 until 1852. The sports included wrestling, leaping, pitching the bar and hammer, handling the pike, walking on the hands, and leapfrog. There was also 'a country dance of Virgins', playing at 'Baloon' (handball), horse-racing, and hunting the hare. Shakespeare has a description of hare-hunting in *Venus and Adonis*, including the animal's death. By order of Robert Dover, a singularly enlightened man for his day, the hare might not be killed at the Cotswold Games. But men were allowed to play kickshins, which speaks for itself – the art of kicking an opponent's shins while wearing iron-tipped, hob-nailed boots. Ilmington men particularly enjoyed it. A pair of these boots were preserved at the White Lion Inn for many years after the sport disappeared. A certain George Wilson, born near Ilmington in 1913, recalled that his grandfather was the last shin-kicking champion at Dover's Games. Shin-kicking was also popular in the local pubs. At the King's Head, Wellesbourne, players used the old rat pit; dog fights were held in it too. The same served as head-quarters for the Warwickshire hunt. But hunting was more sport for the farmers and upper classes than for the ordinary people. A hunting person at Berkswell was so fond of the sport that he sat on a wooden hobby horse to deliver his sermons, or so the rumour went.

Dover's Games were finally suppressed in 1852, because of disorderly behaviour among the spectators. The following account, quoted by W. H. Hutton, makes an interesting comparison with modern football supporters:

My mother at that time [a few years before the closure] used to go to Dover's Hill each year, taking a large tent, a good supply of ale, cider, wine, spirits, and eatables to sell during the gaming week. She made a good sum of money, and the surroundings were so alarming that as fast as her silver changed into gold she would drop the sovereigns into the large barrels of ale or cider through the bung-hole (this was her safety bank). She also had a couple of loaded revolvers under the serving table ready for use. She never left the tent day or night until the festivities were over, as no one was safe from the lawlessness of the crown of card-sharpers, thimble-riggers, pick-pockets, thieves, confidence-men, vagrants, and criminals of the deepest dye, the riff-raff of society. During the daytime the turmoil was terrible, but all night long it was a perfect pandemonium. Cries of murder were often heard, and disorder and rapine held full sway. If the shadow of a person showed through the sheeting of the tent at night he would be almost certain to be struck with a heavy bludgeon from without, and the miscreant would crawl underneath and rob his victim.

Traditional games, so much a feature of these occasions, were played at other times of the year. Bumblepuppy, a form of skittles, was popular at Barston. Quoits, using heavy metal rings, was played on village greens, especially in the late autumn and early winter. Maxstoke and Ilmington were noted for it. A shovel-board table nine feet long is preserved at Maxstoke Castle. The object of this game was to flip a coin with the open hand to a given mark, the winner being the closest. It is still possible to find tables marked out in public houses. There is a tradition that Shakespeare used to play shovel-board at the Falcon in Stratford. Certainly, he mentions the game in *The Merry Wives of Windsor*.

'Put' was played with an elongated cube, its four sides marked P, T, H and L, and the two ends, A and D. This die, called the put — hence the name of the game — was thrown up in turn by the players. If the P came up the thrower had to put a marble in the pool. With the T he took one; with the H he could take half the contents of the pool. L meant 'let 'em alone', and the thrower neither took nor lost any marbles. With D the player had to double the number of marbles in the pool, but A meant take all.

There were other board games like fox and geese and nine men's morris, both extremely popular with farm workers, who sometimes improvised with black and white beans and unusual boards. At Binton there is a fox and geese diagram on the lid of a great corn bin at one farm. There are two boards for nine men's morris at Halford, one cut in the turf, the other on the lid of a corn chest. There is also a diagram in the Lady Chapel of Wixford Church. At Whitchurch it was played in the meadows until within living memory, though bad weather could fill up the holes with mud, a difficulty which Shakespeare knew and mentions in *A Midsummer Night's Dream*. In the gardens behind the Memorial Theatre at Stratford a space for playing the game has been marked out, on a large scale. Miniature versions on sale in the shops could be easily constructed. Here is how Brand describes the game:

In that part of Warwickshire where Shakespeare was educated ... the shepherds and other boys dig up the turf with their knives to represent a sort of imperfect chess-board. It consists of a square, sometimes only a foot diameter, sometimes three or four yards. Within this is another square, every side of which is parallel to the external square; and these squares are joined by lines drawn from each corner of both squares and in the middle of each line. One party, or player, has wooden pegs, the other stones, which they move in such a manner as to take up each other's men, as they are called, and the area of the inner square is called the pound, in which the men taken up are impounded. These figures are by the country people called *nine men's morris* ... ; and are so called because each party has nine men. These figures are always cut upon the green turf, or leys as they are called, or upon the grass at the end of ploughed lands, and in rainy seasons never fail to be choked up with mud.

Mabel Ashby, writing in 1961, remembered wrestling, 'generally between two wrestlers, but still occasionally pick-a-back wrestling in two lines'. There was an annual match of tip-cat played every Good Friday morning between two local sides on St Nicholas' Meadow at Warwick. In spring the farm workers would come out on to the village green, wearing their hob-nailed working boots, to play football 'of a sort'. At Atherstone the football was of the ancient kind, involving a contest between large numbers of people, with very few rules. It is played only on Shrove Tuesdays, and is said to have originated in a match for a bag of gold between the men of Warwickshire and Leicestershire, in the time of King John. More recently the struggle has taken place between different factions from the town itself. This is how the game appeared in the 1960s:

A well-known personality is invited to start the game each year by throwing in the large-sized football (similar to a medicine ball) to the waiting crowds from a first floor window of the Blue Bell Inn, Long Inn (Watling Street). Shops and house windows on the route of the game are boarded up beforehand as a protection against possible damage during the coming fight. The game begins at three o'clock on Shrove Tuesday and finishes at five o'clock. During the course of the match the ball is passed up and down certain streets in the town and frequently lands in the Coventry Canal at the end. After 4.30, and if the players are quick enough, the ball can be deflated and smuggled away till five o'clock when the victor returns, carrying the leather casing. At night the ball used to be blown up again and carried round the town when money was collected mostly for charity, but this is not done now. .... Once the ball was captured at the beginning of the game. This was done by kicking it to the edge of the crowd where an expert runner was waiting to carry it out of town. To avoid this happening again in recent years it has been filled with water, before the game started, which has made it impossible to kick it for more than a few yards at a time. The balls are replaced each year so that the leather casings and also the coloured ribbons can be retained by their respective winners.

This street football is the forerunner of the modern game. William Webb Ellis, traditionally the founder of rugby football, was doing nothing new at Rugby School in 1823 when 'with a fine disregard for the rules of football as played in his time he took the ball in his arms and ran with it'; he was reverting to an earlier style. But we remember Webb as the father of modern rugby, and he is commemorated by a plaque on the Doctor's Wall at the school.

Meriden, in the middle of the ancient Forest of Arden, still has its Company of Woodmen, who practise archery. There is a revival of interest in the sport throughout the country, but the Woodmen can trace their history back to late medieval times. The company lapsed, and was revived in 1785. The diarist and traveller, John Byng, saw them in the Bull's Head at Meriden in 1789, 'all equipp'd in a green uniform, round hats and black feathers'. They used to hold a triennial competition with the Royal Company of Archers, the monarch's bodyguard in Scotland, the matches alternating between Edinburgh and Meriden; a silver bugle was offered as the prize. We are used now to modern revivals of ancient customs, but the revived Company of Woodmen is fast becoming ancient itself.

Other sports disappeared long ago and are only remembered by the occasional phrase or place-name. 'As rough as a bear's backside' and 'as full of meagrims as a dancing bear' are Warwickshire expressions. 'To play the bear' was to inflict heavy damage; Wright gives as an example in his dictionary of dialect, 'The pigs have been in the garden and played the bear with it'. A children's game, called baiting the bear, retained the memory of this old, cruel sport until the last years of the nineteenth century.

> Here lies John Bull:
> If you don't hit him hard, I ull [will]

A group of boys then took it in turn to hit another, who crouched down and used his jacket for protection. The 'bear' had to try and identify one of his assailants, who then took his place.

'As big as bull beef' means pompous, and Birmingham's famous Bull Ring owes its name to one John Cooper, who obtained permission in the time of Henry VIII to bait a bull there. The stake to which the bulls were tied, and the board ring round about, could be seen until late in the nineteenth century. Badger-drawing and bull-baiting were at one time 'everyday occurrences', but bull-baiting in the streets of Birmingham was banned in 1773. The sport, even on private land, was 'discouraged by all well disposed citizens' and by 'the more respectable inhabitants'. Workmen 'of two or three manufactories at a time' got round this by clubbing together and buying a bull for baiting. There would be five or six at every wake.

In 1798, as part of Chapel Wake, a bull bait was arranged behind the Salutation Inn, Snow Hill, now demolished. The Birmingham Loyal Association, 'a body of Volunteer Militia formed by the trading class', was persuaded to intervene. An eye-witness described what happened:

> The Association assembled in the Bull Ring [ironically enough], and marched, with colours flying and drums beating, to the baiting place in Snow Hill. On arriving there they found that the mob, having notice of the attack, had transferred themselves and the bull to Birmingham Heath. Although the day was intolerably hot, the Association gallantly resumed their weary march, and after a due amount of toil reached the scene of action. The bull-baiters scampered off in all directions, taking the dogs with them, but leaving the bull tied to the stake, and the Association leisurely proceeded to secure their formidable prize. A strong cord was made fast to the bull's horns, and tied round his forelegs, the chain was unloosed from the stake, guards were told off, who, with fixed bayonets, reconducted the poor animal in triumph into the town, a vast crowd, of course, 'assisting' at the novel ceremony. The procession passed through the principal streets, and at last the bull was safely lodged in the yard of the

old prison, in Peck Lane. During the night an attempt at rescue was made, but it failed; and for years afterwards the street boys revenged themselves for the disturbance of the sport by singing a song depicting the volunteers in uncomplimentary colours.

Unfortunately, only a fragment of the song has been preserved, telling of those who 'spoiled the wake/And stole the stake/ And took the bull to the Dungeon'. Another song, congratulating the volunteers, was published by a local balladeer, William Mackay. The baitings nevertheless continued. At Chapel Wake in 1811 a bull broke loose, a child was killed, and many people were seriously injured. There was another bull bait at Little Hockley Pool in 1828. The last in the Birmingham area was not until 1838.

The combat between a lion and dogs arranged at Warwick in 1825 by Wombwell's Menagerie was no doubt meant to appeal to a public which enjoyed blood sports. Cock-fighting was another with a wide following. For many years it was accepted practice. 'Fought a cock at Clifford. Won': an entry in the diary of Joseph Hill, a Stratford barber, for 1799. 'Mr Dowel fought two cocks at the Windmill for one guinea each. Won one and lost one. With Joseph Smith'. But many cock fights were much grander affairs. 'County was matched against county, and town against town, with noblemen and magistrates presiding over the combats. They often lasted for several days; great wagers sometimes depended on the results; and even the stakes were often considerable. . . . They began in the morning generally, fighting ten pairs of cocks before dinner, which was also generally a grand affair got up for the occasion, and ten pairs in the afternoon, badger baiting, [more] cock fighting, or pugilism filling up the interval in between'. These gatherings were advertised in the local press, after this style:

Birmingham Cock Match. – On Whitsun Monday, the 8th of June, will be shown at Duddeston Hall, near Birmingham, in Warwickshire, 41 cocks on each side, for a match to be fought the three following days betwixt the gentlemen of Warwickshire, Worcestershire,and Salop for ten guineas a battle.

The fight, which took place in 1747, inspired this poem:

> Where Dudston's walks with vary'd beauty shine,
> And some are pleased with bowling, some with wine,
> Behold a gen'rous train of Cocks repair,
> To vie for glory in the toils of war;
> Each hero burns to conquer or to die:
> What mighty hearts in little bosoms lie!

At length the poet moves on to describe the battle:

> The crested bird, whose voice awakes the morn,
> Whose plumage streaks of radiant gold adorn,
> Proud of his birth on fair *Salopia's* plain,
> Stalks round, and scowls defiance and disdain.

> But, lo! another comes, renown'd for might,
> Renown'd for courage, and provokes the fight.
> Yet what, alas! avails his furious mien,
> His ruddy neck, and breast of varied green?
> Soon thro' his brain the foe's bright weapon flies,
> Eternal darkness shades his swimming eyes;
> Prostrate he falls, and quiv'ring spurns the ground,
> While life indignant issues from the wound.

Then follows the moral conclusion:

> Unhappy hero, had thy humbler life
> Deny'd thee fame by deeds of martial strife,
> Still hadst thou crow'd, for future pleasures spar'd,
> The'exulting monarch of a farmer's yard.
> Like fate, alas! too soon th'illustrious prove,
> The great by hatred fall, the fair by love;
> The wise, the good, can scarce preserve a name,
> Expung'd by envy from the rolls of fame.

Duddeston Hall, formerly the seat of Sir Thomas Holte, and later known as Vauxhall, was not the only place in Birmingham where cockfights might be seen: there was a pit at the Old Crown Inn, Deritend, and new sites were opened at Smallbrook Street in 1809 and Coleshill Street in 1817. One of the first mains (matches) at

Smallbrook Street was 'between the gentlemen of Warwickshire and Staffordshire, for £5 5s the battle, and 100 guineas the main'. The New Pit, as it was called, remained popular until it was closed, in about 1825. 'It was suppressed by the magistrates, who seized about a hundred of the principals and spectators, tied them together, and marched them through the chief streets as an example'. They were then fined. 'To some extent even now', wrote Jaffray in 1855, 'the practice is indulged in. At Shrovetide there are occasionally cock-fights, got up in public house kitchens, which are carefully concealed from the knowledge of the police, though not always successfully.' A Birmingham publican was fined £5 in 1868 for 'unlawfully keeping open his house . . . for the purpose of fighting of cocks'. Tradition has it that cock-fights went on at the White Lion in Digbeth until the 1870s at least.

Outside Birmingham, there is evidence that the sport was widespread throughout the county. No Man's Heath in the north was a popular site for cock-, and later prize-fights, since it was remote from the law. Several counties met nearby, and the 'principals and spectators' could easily move into the next county, even if the police did arrive. From Sutton and Meriden in the north to Halford and Tysoe in the south there are indications that fights took place. At Halford the wooden cockpit survived until recently. At Kenilworth the fights were held at Abbey End, a piece of common land, later used as a slaughter yard. Cockings at Leamington were held on the old bowling green, by the south-west corner of the church, near the Black Dog. At Tysoe traces of a cockpit could be seen on the village green until the 1860s or '70s. There is still, according to a recent guide book, a railed cockpit in the farmhouse at Fell Mill Farm, near Shipston. Polesworth was the home of the Gilliver family, who were noted cock-feeders, or trainers. Joseph, the best known, worked by appointment to King George III and IV. A letter which was merely addressed, we are told, to 'Mr Bill Gilliver, Cock Fighter, England', was duly delivered.

Although it was made illegal in 1849, cock-fighting took a long time to disappear and it left its mark on the language. 'No cocks eyes out' was a Warwickshire expression, meaning 'no great harm has been done, therefore you can get on with whatever you were doing'. 'That cock won't fight' means 'that won't be any good'. 'To quarrel like fighting cocks' is self-evident, so is the current saying, 'To eat like fighting cocks'. 'The fighting cocks' is also a popular name for a public house, and some of the phraseology found its way into prize fighting. The names for different categories — bantam weight, feather weight, and so on — are used to this day. 'No long time since', wrote an indignant parson in 1857, 'Shirley bore an unenviable notoriety for all that was bad and vicious. Within my recollection and during the early years of my ministry, Shirley Street had become the last resort of lovers of brutalising sports. It was here they indulged with impunity and unmolested in bull-baiting, cock-fighting, and pugilistic encounters, and it was here that they found congenial companions'.

Boxing was popular in Warwickshire. Joseph Hill of Stratford wrote in his diary of 5 May 1800.

> Very warm day. Cooks, a maltmaker, and a plumber fought for five guineas each. Cooks won. The plumber fell and [was] knocked down one hundred and eighteen times. The battle lasted two hours and a three-quarters.

In those days a round came to an end only with a knock-down, and the contest ended when a fighter could no longer come to the scratch at the beginning of a new round, hence the expression 'not up to scratch'. Birmingham was an important centre for the sport, and it produced a number of professionals who achieved national fame, men like Ben Caunt, 'Hammer' Lane and Bob Brettle. The last two came from Summer Lane, noted for prize fighters. It retained the reputation of being very tough until the 1930s. The earliest recorded prize fight in Birmingham was in 1782, when a professional called Jemmy Sargent met Isaac Perrins, a Soho workman, for a purse of 100 guineas. 'Jemmy knuckled under after being knocked down thirteen times ... by the knock-kneed hammerman from Soho, whose mates, it is said, won £1,500 in bets through his prowess.' The sport was eventually banned, not because of any danger to the participants, but on account of mass rowdyism among the spectators.

Paradoxically, perhaps, a large town like Birmingham clung tenaciously to the old popular sports. Workmen in the area into late Victorian times insisted on keeping up Saint Monday: the right to take a holiday on Mondays. Prize-fights used to be staged every Monday for this reason, until they were stopped around the middle of the century by the police. The poet, George Davis, writing in 1790, indicates that Saint Monday was noted for eating and drinking, marbles, skittles, quoits, five-balls, plays, opera and variety. Visiting brothels and beating up the watchman were also popular.

During the second half of the nineteenth century, sport and recreation as we know them today were beginning to evolve. Public parks, swimming baths, art galleries and museums were opened. Large-scale, commercially organised sport became a feature. In 1874 Aston Villas, as it then was, came into existence, and in 1875 the Small Heath Alliance, now Birmingham City Football Club, was founded. The Warwickshire County Cricket Club settled in Birmingham in 1885. At the Edgbaston ground one can still here 'Come on Warwick', shouted in a strong Birmingham accent. Indoors the music hall and variety theatre became favourites, with the disappearance of traditional sports.

➡10⬅

March to Wakes and Fairs

ACCORDING to a government survey of 1888 there were eighteen fairs extant in Warwickshire, two more than a century earlier. This indicates a continuation into modern times of an essentially pre-industrial phenomenon. In Birmingham there is evidence that the popularity of fairs was steadily growing with industrialisation, rather than the contrary.

What we loosely call fairs covers at least three types: the fair proper, the hiring fair, and the church wake. The fair proper was an annual occasion, instituted by charter, when goods might be sold. This compares with the market, a weekly occurrence. Often, both fair and market were authorised by a single charter. Aston Cantlow (1204), Bidford (1219-20), Nuneaton (1225-6) and Kineton (1229-30) all had dual charters. Many places held more than one fair in a year. Coleshill (1207-8) had three, and Warwick four.

The purpose and date of these fairs varied from place to place. Until the early eighteenth century cherry wakes were held at Warwick. On three successive Sundays during cherry-picking time, stalls of the fruit were placed along Coten End. The name Cherry Street recalls the cherry wakes; probably it was the site of a former orchard. Cherry wakes were held until fairly recently at Shipston, Shottery, Welford and Stratford. The cherry seller's cry could still be heard in the 1920s:

> Cherry ripe, cherry ripe,
> Some are black and some are white;
> All are fresh gathered from the tree,
> The finest sorts you ever did see,
> Fit for lords, dukes or squires,
> And for the pretty girls to admire;
> But then I didn't come here to amuse you:
> I bring something to put between the nose and chin
> And don't care whether I lose or whether I win.

Birmingham Horse Fair survived until the same period. Its site is still known as Horse Fair, and a mosaic depicts the former scene. David Cox painted it, and perhaps this children's rhyme contains a reference:

> Bunk-eye, squint-eye, went to the fair,
> Bought two horses and one was a mare;
> One was blind and the other couldn't see,
> Bunk-eye, squint-eye, one, two, three.

At Henley there was a cattle and sheep fair on Lady Day (25th March), and a third fair on the eve and day of St Giles (1st September). At the St Giles Fair a Court of Pie Powder, presided over by the steward of the Lord of the Manor, dispensed justice for all who attended. The fair-goers were known as 'pieds poudreux' — dusty feet; hence the name of the court.

Kenilworth had its Crock Fair, every October at Mill End. 'It consisted of one huge stall. The stall-holder was a great character and drew large crowds. He would stand upon a tea chest and thump a chamber pot against its side, shouting that it would stand a ton weight and hold two gallons'. Tanworth in Arden held a cattle fair on the village green on St George's Day (23rd April). All these fairs had small stalls selling a great variety of goods: food and drink, souvenirs, ribbons, household goods, clothes, shoes, ballads, and of course there would be all kinds of side-shows.

Sometimes a trade fair would be combined with a hiring fair. But normally the 'mop' as such fairs were usually called, was mainly for hiring. In Warwickshire they were held in late September or early October, during the slack period after the harvest. Farm labourers and maid-servants wanting to hire out for the coming year assembled on the day, wearing the badge of their trade. 'Mop' is said to derive from the maids' practice of holding miniature mops. An excellent account of these 'statute' fairs, as they were called, was written by a Birmingham correspondent of Hone's *Everyday Book* in 1827:

> The servants were, for the most part, bedecked in their best church-going clothes. The men also wore clean white [smock] frocks, and carried in their hats some emblem or insignia of the situation they had been accustomed to or were desirous to fill: for instance, a waggoner, or ploughboy, had a piece of whipcord in his hat, some of it ingeniously plaited in a variety of ways and entwined round the hatband; a cowman after the same manner had some cow-hair; and to those already mentioned there was occasionally added a piece of sponge; a shepherd had wool; a gardener had flowers....
>
> The girls wishing to be hired were in a spot apart from the men and boys, and all stood not unlike cattle at a fair waiting for dealers. ... Where a master or a mistress was engaged in conversation with a servant they were usually surrounded by a group ... this in some, perhaps, was mere idle curiosity, in others, from desire to know the wages asked and given, as a guide to themselves ... When a bargain is concluded ..., it is the custom to ratify it immediately, and on the spot, by the master presenting to the servant what is termed 'earnest money', which is usually one shilling....
>
> When the hiring is over, the emblems in the hats are exchanged for ribbons of almost every hue. Some retire to the neighbouring grounds to have games at bowls, skittles, or pitching, etc. etc., whilst the more unwary are fleeced of their money by the itinerant Greeks and black legs with E.O. tables, pricking in the garter, the three thimbles, etc. etc. ... Towards

evening each lad seeks his lass, and they hurry off to spend the night at the public-houses. . . . The rooms of the several houses are literally crammed, and usually remain so throughout the night.

The writer obtained his information by visiting mops at Studley, Shipston and Aston Cantlow. The bargaining between farmer and servant is described in a song which was a favourite at Warwickshire harvest homes:

Farmer: Come all you lads that be here for service,
Come here, you jolly dogs:
Who will help me with my harvest,
Milk my cows and feed hogs?

Yonder stands as likely a fellow,
As e'er trod in leathern shoe,
Canst thou plough and canst thou harrow?
Servant: O yes, master! and I can milk too!

Farmer: Here's five pounds in standing wages,
Daily well thou shalt be fed,
With good cabbage, beef and bacon,
Butter-milk, and oaten bread.

Here's a shilling, take it yarnisht, [earnest]
And a Thursday thou must come;
For my servants do all leave me,
And my work it must be done.

Tanworth hiring, again on the green, was on Michaelmas Day (29 September). Hampton Statutes occupied three days, the 'eve, day and morrow of St Luke' (17-19 October). Bidford, Southam, Polesworth and Henley also had mops. The latest in the county seems to have been at Rugby on 11 November; it was combined with a cattle fair, and known as Martlemas Fair. In many places, after a short interval, there was a Runaway Mop which provided those dissatisfied with their earlier agreement with an opportunity to change. Mr Lusby of Wellesbourne was hired as a boy of 11 at Warwick in 1917, the last year when mops — for hiring, that is — were held there.

The first mop in Warwick market place was on 12 October. Then there were two more on the next two Saturdays after. We stood in a row in the market place. . . . The farmer used to come up to us and say, 'Oh, will you come and work for me?' If you said 'yes' he give you the shillin' and you'd start next morning. . . . I had my shillin' but I got talking to some people afterwards and they said: 'The farmer ent worth tuppence'. So, next day, I got the shillin' off my father and I sent it back to the farmer so I didn't go.

Mr Lusby was then able to go to one of the Runaway Mops to try again. Henley has its mop on 11 October and its Runaway Mop, conveniently combined with a hop fair, on the 29th. At Southam there were three runaway mops, on the three successive Mondays after Old Michaelmas Day (10 October). Stratford's Runaway Mop was on 19 October.

Stratford Mop, perhaps the most famous, was held on 12 October. It had begun 'when the mind of man runneth not to the contrary'. The entertainments included morris dancing, climbing a greasy pole, ducking for sixpences, and grinning through a horse collar. Grinning – 'the frightfullest grinner to be winner' – seems to have been a particular favourite in Warwickshire. One of the attractions at the horse races on Coleshill Heath in 1711 was a grinning competition with a gold ring as prize. The *Spectator* commented:

The Prize which is proposed to be grinn'd for, has raised such an Ambition among the Common People of Out-grinning one another, that many very discerning Persons are afraid it should spoil most of the Faces in the County; and that a *Warwickshire* Man will be known by his Grinn, as Roman Catholics imagine a *Kentish* Man by his Tail.

John Byng saw a crowd assembled at Henley-in-Arden when he was passing through in 1792. 'Two fellows upon stools' were 'grinning for a wager (a sport I thought disused).'

Catching a pig by its greasy tail, another Stratford competition, was not at all easy: the pig was the prize. There were also what we now call barbecues. 'At Stratford-upon-Avon', wrote a schoolboy on

17 October 1875, 'there was a mop. Three oxen and two pigs were roasted whole in the street. There was a lot of shooting galleries and shows; I went into one show and saw a man swallow two swords; I am sure he did. There were also two waggon horses, 21 hands high!' Others were not so pleased. In September 1877 the local newspaper commented on 'the usual debaucheries of so-called enjoyment' at Kenilworth and here is a report from King's Norton:

The King's Norton Saturnalia is growing worse. Hardly a man or women with any pretension to self-respect could be seen at the Mop last Monday, and the thousands were composed of shouting hobbledehoys, screaming girls, drunken men, and shouting women. They swarmed from the station in hundreds during the day, and as night drew on the crushing, the swearing, created indescribable confusion. A great mass of people stood round the roasting ox, which had been frizzling all night before a huge fire and then was cut up for the delectation of the crowd. A basket of slices of bread stood near, and two or three hot red-faced men with carving knives, sliced away at the haunches, the ribs, and the shoulders, putting a slice of meat between two slices of bread and selling the tasty morsels at four pence a piece. The public houses were packed and customers had to fight their way in and out, treading on floors wet with slopped beer. Some disgraceful scenes took place in one part or another of the vicinity during the day and night. The general proceedings offered a spectacle of debauchery, drunkenness, noise and blasphemy, in strong contrast to the ordinary quiet life of King's Norton.

This article was part of a campaign which eventually led to the suppression of King's Norton Mop – though it was revived in 1953. Other mops gradually disappeared and the 1914-18 war put an end to them. Many still flourish, like the one at Stratford, though their function is solely for pleasure.

The wake was originally a vigil to honour the patron saint of a particular church, which gradually changed into a secular event. Trinity Sunday is the patronal festival at Long Itchington: a fair opens on the village green the previous day. During the rest of wakes week householders observed the custom of leaving two dishes on the sideboard for every visitor. One contained stuffed chine, the other, wake pudding – a sort of bread-pudding made of thin layers of bread and currants, with eggs, milk, sugar, suet and peel. Alderminister held its patronal festival on Whit Monday: the wake began the previous day and lasted for a week. On Monday the men bowled for a leg of mutton: on Tuesday there was a dancing; on Wednesday it was the turn of the women to bowl for a currant cake. Then they adjourned to the Bell for drinking and dancing. A man who went into the parlour was seized and held by the women until he paid a sixpenny fine. Newbold celebrated on the feast of Saint Philip and Saint James (1 May). At Wootton Wawen the maypole set up in front of the Bull's Head on 1st May was taken down on Wake Day (29 June).

Bearley Wakes began on Whit Sunday, lasted for two or three days, and were followed by Snitterfield. Quinton began on Whit Sunday, Tredington on St Agatha's Day (28 June), Shottery on the first Tuesday in July, and Aston Cantlow on the second Sunday in July. Whatcot was on the 11th and Ettington on the 18th July. Of these, Aston Cantlow, which lasted a week, was the most important. the sports included donkey, wheelbarrow, and sack races, swordplay, wrestling, bowling, and all-night dancing. At Ilmington there was a wake at the Fox on the second Sunday in October, with badger-baiting; this sport was popular at Ilmington, where the dogs were renowed for their courage. Nearby Meon Hill Wake was noted for bull-baiting: blood sports were very much a feature of the wakes.

In Birmingham, apart from the horse fair mentioned earlier, there were three principal wakes and two main fairs. Deritend Wake, inaugurated in 1383, was held on St John's Day (29 August), when 'it was the custom to carry bulrushes to the church, and old inhabitants decorated their fireplaces with them'. Chapel Wake began in 1750, when St Bartholomew's Chapel was opened. Bell Wake was held on 24 August in the following year to mark the hanging of ten bells in St Philip's Church. In September and October there were smaller wakes in the surrounding villages of Edgbaston, Handsworth, Moseley (remembered in the present street name, Wake Green Road), St George's, and Ashted.

William Hutton, the Birmingham historian was scathing about the wakes: 'the lowest of all low amusements, and compleatly suited to the lowest of tempers'. He complained that 'the devotional part is forgot, the church is deserted, and the festivity turned into a riot, drunkenness, and mischief'. Chapel Wake 'was hatched and fostered by the publicans, for the benefit of the spiggot'. Bell Wake was celebrated with bull-baiting and horse-racing through the streets. At St Philip's Wake naked boys raced through the streets. Hutton approvingly notes that some townsfolk, 'seeing so fair a mark for chastisement, applied the rod with success, and put a period to that unseemly sport'.

Jaffray wrote in 1855 that the wakes were, 'as they are too often now, scenes of the grossest cruelty, absurdity, and debauchery'. He mentions grinning through collars, eating hasty pudding scalding hot, and running in sacks as 'the most innocent of these amusements!' A favourite and cruel sport involved 'tying a live goose on the centre of a rope, which stretched from one side of the street to the other, and attempting to pull the head of the poor bird off as horsemen galloped beneath'. Jaffray refers to 'smock races in the streets by women for gowns and pounds of tea' and to the races of boys 'in a state of nudity . . . through the principal thoroughfares. . . . Even men, also nude, bedaubed with treacle, and sometimes feathered, were seen competing for prizes in the principal streets of the town. One of these fellows, as late as 1809, was apprehended, sent to prison, and flogged at the cart's tail; another was sentenced to a year's imprisonment, and stood in the pillory.' But everything turned out all right in the end: 'These disgusting scenes were never repeated. The wakes and fairs of the present day are celebrated chiefly by drinking and sight-seeing, and only the humbler classes participate in them'.

In contrast to the wakes, the Birmingham fairs 'are at this day in great repute' — so Hutton wrote at the beginning of the nineteenth century. The Whitsun Fair originated in 1251, when William de Birmingham, the Lord of the Manor, obtained a charter from Henry III. Originally the fair began on the eve of Holy Thursday, and lasted four days, but in 1752 it was moved, and opened on the Thursday in Whitsun week, so that 'less time might be lost to the injury of work and the workman'. The other fair, lasting three days, began on the eve of St Michael's Day (29 September). Both fairs were mainly for pleasure, though the second became known as the Onion Fair, since it was popular with onion-growers from Buckinghamshire. They were opened with due civic dignity. A procession of fair-walkers toured the town, stopping at various points to proclaim the fairs. The Town Crier rang his bell, and there was a band, the High and Low Bailiffs, 'many of the principal inhabitants', and small boys. In 1825 grotesque figures appeared, but in 1851 the civic procession took place for the last time. The fairs, however, continued, and increased in popularity. Vast numbers of people from Birmingham were joined by miners from the Black Country and many others from the surrounding countryside. Wombwell's managerie and band were always popular and the dramatic entertainment provided in the tent theatres was much appreciated. 'At night crowds incessantly pour up', wrote the *Birmingham Journal* in 1851; 'there is a performance every seven minutes; and the drama is triumphant.'

> *The Red Robber's Revenge* was enacted with the greatest *éclat* in the astonishing space of five minutes, the chief incident being a terrific combat between the Blood Thirsty Baron and the Red Robber, in which the former was routed with great slaughter. Then followed a comic song which affected everybody to tears, and a one-act pantomime in which the clown tumbled three somersets, knocked Harlequin down twice, pulled his nose, and then suggested that the performance was finished, an announcement strongly protested against on the ground that nobody had got enough for their money.

The show tents were usually pitched in Dale End and Smithfield, stalls and booths in Dale End and the lower part of Bull Street, the whole of High Street, part of New Street, the Bull Ring, Digbeth as far as Allison Street, Spiceal Street, Jamaica Row, and the whole of Smithfield. This meant that twice a year a large part of the town centre was taken over for several days, by the fairs. As time went on, tradesmen and shopkeepers supported the fairs; industrialists and moralists campaigned against them. They said that the fairs were 'a hindrance to trade, and a cause of annoyance to sober and quiet people'; at night there were noisy, 'dissipated, and drunken crowds'. Prostitution was a problem too.

From 1861 the Town Council limited the fairs to the Bull Ring and the upper part of Digbeth and Smithfield, while the pleasure shows and theatrical booths were confined to Smithfield. In

September 1874, the *Birmingham Post* printed this lively description of the autumn fair:

Birmingham Onion Fair commenced yesterday with no signs whatever of decaying vitality, and will continue until midnight on Saturday. Contrary to old established tradition, the weather was fine and excursion trains from all directions brought thousands of visitors into the town. The sale of onions was, as usual, very little more than an excuse for the Fair.

The collection of shows which took possession of the ground as soon as the business in the cattle market was over was of about the usual magnitude and, notwithstanding the warnings that have been circulated about the danger of taking smallpox, the crush was as great as ever. The Bull Ring is occupied, as on previous occasions, by cake, gingerbread and toy stalls, peepshows, 'art studios', and the Bible Stall, while in Smithfield and Jamaica Row are to be found the more spacious exhibitions with their attendant swing boats, the more spacious shooting galleries, instruments for the trial of physical strength and the like. The principal show is Wombwell's Royal Windsor Castle Managerie, which appears still to be carried on with some considerable enterprise. Among recent additions are two very fine Rangoon elephants : making four distinct varieties of elephant to be seen at the exhibition. The Indian rhinoceros has now gained its full growth and is an extremely fine specimen.

Mrs Edmun's collection will well repay a visit. In addition to this, there is a Day's Menagerie, Holden and Radford's marionettes, a circus, two moving waxwork shows, Miss Anderson's Temple of Magic, Laurence's working models, an establishment devoted to the 'manly art of self-defence', a champion skittle-bowler who never fails to knock down the whole nine pins, a conjuror who swallows a sword, and a large variety of giants, dwarves, fat women and animal monstrosities.

In spite — or because of — this popular appeal, the anti-fair party won the day. In June 1875 after an angry debate the council agreed to prohibit the use of the land and streets for the fairs. The showmen moved outside the city boundary to a piece of land near Aston Church, called the Old Pleck. The Onion Fair was still held there in the 1930s, and one of the showmen's cries is well remembered: 'Walk up! Walk up! ladies and gentlemen! just a-going to begin! Only one penny to the gallery! So be in time! Walk up! Walk up!' Gradually the famous fair turned into an ordinary event. The distance from the centre of the town would not have helped, but the main enemy seems to have been respectability, combined with the new forms of organised sport and entertainment.

The story could be repeated, with variations, in many other towns. Coventry had four fairs a year: on the second Friday after Ash Wednesday, for the sale of linen and woollen cloth; on the 2nd of May; in June, eight days of revelry which included the famous procession of Lady Godiva. and, finally, on the 2nd of November, for the sale of linen, wool, and horses. 'Few provincial fairs', wrote Hackwood, in *Olden Warwickshire*, 'were so popular in old England as the Coventry Fairs.' They nevertheless declined, though the processions managed to last until the 1960s, thanks to Lady Godiva – but that is another story.

⊃11⊂

Guy and
Godiva

SIR GUY of Warwick and Lady Godiva of Coventry are two of the best-known figures in Warwickshire folklore. Indeed, Sir Guy had an international reputation. A book published in 1562 lists him along with Caesar, King Arthur, Charlemagne and Alexander, as one of the nine worthies of the world. Thirty years later, a set of twelve silver-gilt spoons, decorated with miniature figures of kings and heroes, included Sir Guy. The spoons still exist, and were acquired for £85,000 in 1975 by the Hampshire County Council Museum Service, partly because of Sir Guy's connection with Winchester. The work of Christopher Wace, they are known as the Tichborne Celebrities.

Sir Guy is reputed to have lived in Saxon times, in the reign of King Athelstan, who died in 939. He set out from Warwick, being 'in faith of Christ a christyan true' to win fame by 'feates of armes in strange and sundry heathen lands'. He helped the Emperor of Greece to fight the Sultan's army of Persians and Saracens and killed 'manye a man', including the Sultan's cousin. On an embassy

131

to the Sultan, Guy – treacherously one would have thought – killed him in his tent and 'brought his head awaye'. A dragon unlucky enough to cross his path, was soon dealt with. He then returned to England, and on the journey killed the Duke of Pavia for 'hainous' but unspecified treason. Back at Warwick, he 'wedd faire Phelis' (Phyllis), the earl's daughter. Guy, the son of a steward, was of humble origin. No doubt his feats of arms were designed to convince the earl that he was worthy to marry his daughter.

Forty days after the wedding Guy set off for the Holy Land 'all cladd in grey, in pilgrim sort'. He rescued Earl Jonas and his fifteen sons, who were prisoners of the Saracens. On the way home, Guy killed a giant, Amarant, and called again at Pavia, this time slaying a knight named Barnard. Back in England he found invading Danes encamped outside Winchester, and it was agreed that he would represent England against the Danish champion, Colbrand. Helped by a friendly crow, which flew round the giant's head and confused him, Guy killed his opponent. In 993 there was in fact a joint Norwegian and Danish invasion of the southern counties, but Winchester was saved by payment of money and not by a champion in single combat.

Guy also saved his countrymen from a great wild boar and a dragon. His combat with the Dun Cow was in Warwickshire, at Dunsmore Heath. The animal was a large and benign creature, which gave milk freely to all who came. But she was transformed into a wild fury by greedy, malicious people who milked her into a sieve and exhausted her supply. In his old age Guy returned to Warwick and lived in a cave, unknown. Every day he begged for food at the castle and was given it by his wife, who did not recognise him. When he was dying he sent her a ring, which identified him, and she was present at his death-bed.

The story has elements of romantic love, adventure, patriotism, and piety. The earliest written version is a thirteenth century manuscript in Norman-French metrical verse. The Dun Cow did not appear in this, and other early manuscripts, nor in the early printed editions: the first, also in French, was published in Paris in 1525. The first printed edition in English appeared in early Elizabethan times, entitled *The Booke of the Most Victoryous Prince Guy of Warwick*. The writer of the *Arte of English Poesie* in 1589 contemptuously refers to the 'blind harpers, or such like taverne minstrels that give a fit of mirth for a groat'. Their repertoire included the tale of Sir Guy, 'and such other old romances or historical rhimes, made purposely for the recreation of the common people at Christmas dinners and bride ales, and in tavernes and alehouses, and such other places of base resort'.

Clearly, whatever monkish or aristocratic appeal the story had, it also delighted the common people. It was entered in the Stationers' Register as a street ballad in 1592, was reprinted many times, both as a ballad and a chapbook, and remained popular until the mid-nineteenth century. By then Guy was still enough of a hero to feature in a Birmingham street ballad, extolling the virtues of the local brew:

Of Guy Earl of Warwick our country can boast,
Who in fighting and thumping ruled lord of the roast;
He with courage resistless his foes did assail,
For he strengthened his sinews with Birmingham ale.

The last full version of the ballad of Sir Guy appeared in the 1860s, in *The Universal Melodist*, a popular song book.

Warwickshire variants of the story must have been helped along by numbers of supposed relics. A Dr Caius saw what he took to be a huge cow's head and some vertebrae $7\frac{1}{4}$ inches in circumference at Warwick Castle, a rib over six feet long and 9 inches round in Guy's Chapel at Guy's Cliffe, and an animal's blade-bone, some three feet broad and five feet long, hanging from the north gate at Coventry. He saw these in 1552 and described them in a Latin work in 1579, this being the first mention in print of the Dun Cow. But the story of the cow was not completed until the seventeenth century, when it was brought into a play performed in 1661, said to have been written by Ben Jonson, who died in 1637. The earliest prose account of the cow appeared in 1703. A Dun Cow Inn existed at Dunchurch as early as 1655, and is still there. There was also a Blue Boar Inn at Dunchurch, near which was the Dun Cow's Thicket. At Snitterfield there was, and still is, a Dun Cow Lane.

When John Evelyn, the diarist, visited Warwick in 1654 he was taken to the castle. 'Here they shew us Sir Guy's great two-handed sword, staff, house armes, pott, and other reliques of that famous knight-errant. Hence to Sir Guy's Grot [Guy's Cliffe]. Neere this we were shew'd his chapell and gigantic statue, hewn out of the solid rock. The next place to Coventry. At going forth the Gate they shew us the bone or rib of a wild boare, said to have been kill'd by Sir Guy, but which I take to be the chine of a whale'.

These relics associated with Sir Guy have a bewildering variety of origins. The blade-bone may have come from a mammoth, rather than from a whale. It eventually became the sign of an inn named after it, located between Rugby and Lawford. At Guy's Cliffe there was a chapel built by Richard Beauchamp, Earl of Warwick, in 1422. This was later destroyed, and the present house built on the site in the eighteenth century. In its chapel stands the statue of Sir Guy, eight feet high and six hundred years old. His sandstone cave can still be seen, and the point where Phillis jumped to her death in the Avon, two weeks after he died is known illogically, as Guy's Leap. His armour and accoutrements in Warwick Castle consist of a headpiece (dating from the time of Edward III), a shield (Henry VII), another shield (really a backplate from the time of James I), a two-handed sword, five and a half feet long (Henry VIII), 'the slippers of Phyllis' (pointed iron stirrups from the time of Henry VI), and Guy's walking stick (the shaft of a tilting lance). The horse-armour dates from the time of Henry VI, and 'Guy's porridge pot' is a huge iron cauldron.

Today, Sir Guy and his exploits are little known, but every passer-by in Coventry – and indeed, much further afield – knows the story of Lady Godiva, who rode naked through the town so that her husband would ease the local taxes. Everyone stayed indoors, and refrained from looking, except Peeping Tom, who was struck blind as a punishment. The people of Coventry have an affection for Godiva, and still look on her as a benefactress.

There are historical records of both Godiva and her husband, Leofric. As Earl of Mercia, Leofric ruled vast areas of Midland England. He died in 1057. There is no record of when he married Godiva, but their names were coupled in 1035. Godiva is shown in the Domesday Book as a major Warwickshire landowner. She died in 1067. They founded an abbey in Coventry, which was lavishly endowed, and were responsible for other benefactions. There is no record that they lived in Coventry, but they might have done so between 1038 and 1057. The chronicler Florence of Worcester (died 1118) mentions both Leofric and Godiva with respect, but does not refer to the ride. The earliest extant account is in the *Chronicles* of Roger of Wendover (died 1236), under the year 1057:

> The saintly countess, however, desiring to free the town of Coventry from its burdensome and shameful servitude, often besought the earl, her husband, with earnest prayers, to free the town, by the guidance of the Holy Trinity and of the Holy Mother of God, from this slavery. The earl upbraided her for vainly seeking something so injurious to him and repeatedly forbade her to approach him again on the subject. Nevertheless in her feminine pertinacity she exasperated her husband with her unceasing request and extorted from him the following reply: 'Mount your horse naked', he said, 'and ride through the market place of the town, from one side right to the other, while the people are congregated, and when you return you shall claim what you desire.' And the countess answered: 'And if I wish to do this, will you give me your permission?' And the earl said: 'I will.' Then the Countess Godiva, beloved of God, on a certain day, as it is said, mounting her horse naked, loosed her hair from its bands and her whole body was veiled except her fair white legs. Her journey done, unseen by a soul, she returned rejoicing to her husband, who counted it a miracle. Then Earl Leofric granted a charter freeing the city of Coventry from its servitude and confirmed it with his seal.

A second version of the Wendover text makes it clear that the 'servitude' mentioned was a toll. As Joan Lancaster, the authority on Lady Godiva, points out, this cannot have been merely a local tax, since Godiva would have had the power to remit this herself. The most oppressive tax at the time, the *Heregeld*, was abolished by Edward the Confessor in 1051. There is a possibility that, through her husband, Godiva obtained the remittance of this tax for Coventry before it was lifted throughout the nation.

Some fourteenth-century chroniclers repeat the story, with the variation that Godiva freed the town from all the tolls, except for the one on horses. In none of these sources is there any reference to Peeping Tom. Nor is he mentioned in the ballad version of 1631, or in Dugdale's *Antiquities of Warwickshire,* published in 1656.

Dugdale was a pupil at the King Henry VIII School in Coventry, and had relatives in the city. He would therefore have been likely to know this part of the story. The first written reference to Peeping Tom dates from the latter half of the seventeenth century, but since then he has become a part of the story. Various artefacts have encouraged the tradition. The best-known is a wooden figure, carved in about 1600, and said to represent him. It has what appears to be sightless eyes and an agonised expression. After many years in various houses in Coventry, it is now kept in the Leofric Hotel. The Coventry show fairs were another important element in the growth of the Godiva story.

Coventry's Great Fair dates back to 1218, when Henry III granted a charter to Ranulph III, Earl of Chester, to hold an annual eight-day Trinity Fair. This was an important event for many centuries. By the end of the fifteenth century it was opened by a ceremonial civic procession, in which the mayor led representatives of the various crafts. In 1678 Lady Godiva, joined the procession for the first time, and gradually became the chief attraction. In 1678 'the son of James Swinnerton' took the part of Godiva. By 1765, a real woman was playing the role for a fee of fifteen shillings. This had risen to £5 in 1813; by then the processions had become very elaborate. Here is the order of march for 1809:

GRAND PROCESSION
OF
THE SHOW FAIR

Through Hay-lane, Little Park-street, St. John's-street, Much Park-street, where the fair was proclaimed; Jordanwell, Gosford-street, where the fair was proclaimed; Far Gosford-street, High-street, where the Bablake boys sang; Spon-street, West Orchard, where the Bablake boys sang; Well-street, Bishop-street, Cross Cheaping, where the Bablake boys sang; High-street, and returned through Hay-lane, to Trinity Church-yard.

Twelve Guards — two and two.

SAINT GEORGE,
IN ARMOUR.
TWO BUGLE HORNS.
City Streamers
Two City Followers

City Streamer.

Grand Band of Music, belonging to the 14th Lt. Dragoons.

High Constable
LADY GODIVA
City Cryer and Beadle on each side.
Mayor's Cryer
City Bailiffs
City Maces.
SWORD AND MACE
Mayor's Followers
The Right Worshipful
THE MAYOR
ALDERMEN
Sheriffs Followers.
SHERIFFS.
Common Council
Chamberlains and Followers.
Wardens and Followers.
GRAND BAND OF MUSIC,
Belonging to the 1st Regiment of Warwickshire Local Militia.
COMPANIES.
Mercers — Streamer, Master, and Follower.
Drapers — Streamer, Master, and Followers
Clothiers — Streamer, Master, and Follower
Four Drums and Fifes
Blacksmiths — Streamer, Master, and Follower.
Taylors — Streamer, Master, and Follower
Cappers — Streamer, Master, and Follower
Butchers — Streamer, Master, and Followers.
GRAND BAND OF MUSIC,
Belonging to the Stonely Volunteers
Fellmongers — Streamer, Master, and Followers
Carpenters — Streamer, Master, and Follower
Cordwainers — Streamer, Master, and Follower
Four Drums and Fifes.
Bakers — Streamer, Master, and Follower
Weavers — Streamer, Master, and Follower
Silk Weaver — Streamer, Master, and Follower
Grand Band of Music

Woolcombers – Streamer, Master, and Follower
SHEPHERD AND SHEPHERDESS,
With a Dog, Lamb, etc.
JASON,
With a Golden Fleece, and drawn Sword
Five Wool Sorters.
BISHOP BLAZE
AND WOOLCOMBERS,
In their respective uniforms
FOUR DRUMS AND FIFES

In 1829 the mayor and his officers took part in the procession
for the last time. But it continued, with interest centering more and
more on Godiva herself. Actresses and dancers were usually
engaged to play the part. They wore scanty garments – at least for
the time: tight-fitting dresses, 'fleshings and drapery', 'tights, stays,
white boots, and a tiara' – and there were constant rumours that *this*
year Lady Godiva would appear looking like her original, which
always ensured a good turn-out. There were many controversies. In
1845 the Bishop of Worcester protested against 'a Birmingham
whore being paraded through the streets as Queen Godiva'. In
1854 there were two, rival Godivas. In 1858 the main centre of
the fair was moved from Grey Friars Green further out of town.
The processions were held, in spite of trouble and disapproval, until
the 1960s. They were 'essentially popular, down-to-earth occasions,
rich in local tradition, humour and ribaldry, often rowdyism', says
Joan Lancaster. They were almost unique to Coventry, but there
was one parallel. At nearby Southam in the late eighteenth and early
nineteenth centuries – up to about 1840 – there was a procession
with two Godivas, one white and one black. 'Southam Great Show
Fair', said a newspaper advertisement, quoted by Burbidge,

> will be held on Monday and Tuesday next, the 19th and 20th
> days of May instant, for which greater preparations are now
> making than ever before known, including a Lady Godiva with
> her attendants; a black lady, being a native of the Indies; Bishop
> Blaize and his attendants; a number of children, elegantly dressed
> and decorated, with banners; the grand troupe of equestrian
> horsemen from London with bands of music, and an immense
> number of curiosities too numerous to be inserted.

Another account also quoted by Burbidge, indicates that the procession was headed by 'Old Brazen Face' — a man wearing a bull's mask — and included Peeping Tom 'on horseback in a box frame representing a house and windows'. The Southam processions were suppressed because they were allegedly too rowdy.

Lady Godiva was a brave and generous woman who helped the people of her town, and her processions provided lively entertainment. Underlying the story is a strong hint of sexuality, and this was increasingly less well-received as time went by. Hence the suppression at Southam and the long controversy at Coventry. Today Godiva is very much alive. She features in a long series of pictures, books and critical works. The most recent of many plays was *The only true story of Lady Godiva,* staged at the Belgrade Theatre, Coventry, in 1974. Lady Godiva rode a motor bike, but at last, like the original, she rode naked.

— 12 —

Songs of all Sizes

THE BALLAD singer used to be a popular figure at fairs and markets, and in streets and lanes. Perhaps the earliest Warwickshire reference is in Laneham's *Letter from Kenilworth*. In 1575 one of the performers at an entertainment for Queen Elizabeth was a Coventry mason, Captain Cox. He was a skilled fencer, and knowledgeable in 'storie', 'poetrie', 'auncient playz', 'ballets & songs, all auncient'. He apparently knew a hundred 'ballets, (ballads) and songs; unfortunately Laneham only listed seven.

Like most of the other performers at Kenilworth, Captain Cox seems to have been a part-time professional. Another singer described by Laneham was probably fully professional. His mannerisms recall some of the folk singers of today: 'Appecrez, then loly cooursiez [lowly curtsies], cleered his vois with a hem and a reach, and spat oout withal, wiped his lips with the hollo of his hand, for fyling [to prevent fouling] his napkin, tempered a string or two with his wreast, and after a little warbling on his harp for a prelude, come foorth with a sollem song, warranted for a story oout of King Arthurs acts: "So it befell upon a Penticost day" '

There is another professional performer in *The Winter's Tale*, probably first performed in 1611. Autolycus 'sings several tunes faster than you'll tell money; . . . he hath songs for man or woman, of all sizes'. His pack was filled with 'what maids lack from head to heel' — pins, perfume, gloves, ribbons, and so on. There is nothing which specifically links Autolycus with Warwickshire, but Shakespeare must have seen similar pedlars in his native county.

Not all ballads were sold or produced professionally. We are told that, in the seventeenth century, individuals were constantly held up to ridicule in songs and ballads that were secretly posted, or sometimes printed and spread broadcast. For example, Shakespeare's verses on Sir Thomas Lucy. Inevitably, such material was often short-lived, but in one instance at least, court proceedings have preserved part of a 'libel' by 'one Colmer against Thos. Smalebrooke, a mercer in Bremingham, for his manner of buying and selling, usury, etc.', which ended:

Read now my frindes who this catchpoole should be,
The steward of the towne in plaine tearnes tys hee;
Smalebrooke by name, a brooke that yeldes no fish,
But froggs and toads, and that's no deynty dishe.

Warwickshire balladry, in printed or oral form, is difficult to trace in the seventeenth and eighteenth centuries. There is little evidence of ballad printing in the county in the seventeenth century; presumably supplies came from elsewhere. In the late eighteenth and early nineteenth centuries, J. Turner of High Street, Coventry, was printing ballads; some had been in existence for a century or more. *Death and the lady*, *The famous flower of servingmen*, and *The Oxfordshire tragedy* are some of his many titles. They were part of a national stock of ballads sung in Warwickshire, but not peculiar to the county.

Some ballads clearly originated in Warwickshire, though they circulated further afield — *The button-maker's complaint*, for example:

In Birmingham I liv'd 'tis true,
Where many people did me know;
A Button-maker by my trade,
Tho' I was ruin'd by a maid.

This is a typically eighteenth-century ballad slip, $3\frac{1}{2}$ inches wide, and 12 inches deep, without imprint. 'For getting of a maid with child', the eponymous hero is taken via Knowle to Warwick, and lodged in the gaol. At least for him, there was a happy ending:

> But thanks to God I am out again,
> And on the road a steering,
> Trade it was bad when we poor lads
> Set out a privateering.

There is at least one version in which two of the place-names are garbled, Knowle becomes Null and Warwick, Stolock – an indication that this ballad circulated beyond Warwickshire.

Songs like this were widely disseminated by the ballad-sellers, who were strongly criticised by the authorities. There was a complaint at Polesworth Statutes in 1784 that 'the principal nuisance ... arises from a parcel of balladsingers, disseminating sentiments of dissipation in minds which ought to be trained to industry and frugality.' 'A ballad', continued the writer, 'goes a great way towards forming the morals of rustics; and if, instead of the trash which is everywhere, at present, dealt out at all their meetings, songs in praise of conjugal affection, and a rural life, were substituted, happy effects might ensue.' In Birmingham they were prepared to stand no nonsense for a similar 'nuisance', as a notice made clear: 'The officers of this Town give this public Notice, that they are come to a determined Resolution to apprehend all strolling Beggars, Ballad Singers, and other Vagrants found within this Parish.'

This did not prevent some thirty printers in Birmingham alone from issuing, and presumably selling, some 15,000 titles during the next seventy-five years. At the extremely conservative estimate of 500 copies per title, this means a sale of 7,500,000 ballads. Joseph Russell, whose presses were at work from about 1814 until 1839, advertised 'A general Assortment of Children's Books, School Books, and Account Books, constantly on Sale at the Lowest Wholesale Prices', and 'Slip Songs, Printed and Sold Wholesale and Retail'. An incomplete list shows 139 broadside sheets, with a total of 263 titles. Russell did well enough from his business, and left the considerable fortune of £12,000.

LIST

Of Slip Songs,

Printed and Sold Wholesale and Retail,

BY JOSEPH RUSSELL,

21, Moor Street, Birmingham.

Adieu my native land & Post Captain
Adventures of Little Mike & Young Napoleon, or the Bunch of Roses
Arthur o' Bradley 4to
A Courting I went & Lubin's Cot
Anchor's Weighed & Poor Mary Anne
Bessy the Sailor's Bride & When Pensive I thought on my Love
Boys Water & Susan My Dear
Bonny Hodge & Coal Hole
Banks of Dee & Grand Conversation
Bachelor's Lessons 4to.
Bewildered Maid & down in our Village
Birds of a Feather & the Maid of Judah
Bill Brown & Bristol 'Prentice Boy
Birmingham Boy in London & The Wanderer
Black Eyed Susan 4to.
Blanch Frigate & Gosport Beach
Bloom is on the Rye & Welch Harper
Bonny Lass I love &c. & I Can't find Brumagem
Boys of Kilkenny & Devil & Little Mike
Bold Robin Hood 4to.
Brave Nell 4to.
Brave Nelson & Strephon on the Hill
Bruce's Address &c. & Cottager's Daughter
Butter & Cheese & Valley below
Caledonian Maid & Mary's Dream
Comforts of Man & Drunken Husband
Dream of Napoleon—The Sailor's Love
Dame Durden—Tarry Sailor
Death of General Moore—Fly from the World
Don't be addicted to Drinking & those evening Bells
Darlaston Wake Bull Baiting 4to.
Dandy Wife & Teddy the Tyler
Dandy Husband & Philadelphia Lass
Dawning of the Day & Oyster Girl
Death of General Wolfe & Betsey o' Dundee
Death of Parker & Battle of the Nile
Death of Nelson & Blind Beggars Daughter
Dooting old Man & Nan of the Valley
Dolly Dobbs & Jones a great—
Draw the Sword of Scotland & John Anderson My Jo
Enniskillen Dragoon & Young Henry of the Raging Main
Female Drummer—Daughter of Israel
Farewell to the Mountain & Holy Friar
Flora the Lily of the West & Bridal Ring
Fair Susan & the Cholie
Farmer's Son & Blow the Candle Out
Female Sailor 4to.
Female Smuggler 4to.
Feathers old Sow & Polly Oliver
Flow on Shining River & Sun that Lights &c
Forester's Daughter & Sons of Albion
Gipsey Laddy & Free and Easy
Golden Gate & Unlucky Fellow
George Barnwell 4to.
Glasses Sparkle, Maid of Llangollen & Highland Mary
Green Out a Shooting 4to.
Gold in Glove & Downhill of Life
Green Hills of Tyrol & Blue Mussells
High Mettled Racer & Bold Privateer
Harry Bluff & it Blew Great Guns &c.
Haden the Fair & Streams of Lovely Nancy
Hole in her Stocking & Song about Nothing
How, When & Where & Shepherd Boy
I Wonder where the Money goes & Jack of all Trades
Isle of Beauty & Village Fair
Isle of St. Helena & Burn's Farewell
I've been Roaming & Southern Breezes
Jack Robinson & Giles Scroggin's Ghost
Jim Crow! 4to.

Jack o' Hazeldean & O! merry row the Bonny Bark
Jockey to the Fair & Sweet Silver Moon
Jonny to the Fair 4to.
King Death & I'm too Little for anything
Kitty Jones & Henry's Departure to the Spanish War
Leicester Chambermaid & Lass I Love so Well
Lad with Carrotty Pole & Old King Cole
Law & Old Parson
Leather Breeches 4to.
London 'Prentice Boy & I Never Sarves a Hanimal so
Lord Marlborough & True Lovers or Kings Command
Love in Long-Acre & Lovely Joan
Lubin & Mary & Nothing at all
Maid of Judah & Banks of Allan-Water
Mary-le-more & Fisherman's Boy
May-Pole, Besom maker & Light-Horse Man, slain in the Wars
Mistletoe Bough & Follow the Drum
My own Blue-Bell, Light Guitar, My Native Hills & Last Rose of Summer
New Garden Fields—Fly away pretty Moth
New York Streets & Lamentations of an old Horse
Nothing & One Bottle More
Not a Drum was Heard & Fly from the World
Old Mr. December—When I was out a Drinking
Oh, no we never mention Her, I stood amidst the Glittering throng & he that will not Merry be
Old England come to & Billy o' Rook's the Boy Sir
On the Banks of the River & New Song called true Lovers
Overseer outwitted & Faithful lovers or, hero rewarded
Paddy's Blunder 4to.
Plains of Waterloo 4to.
Pretty Susan the Pride of Kildare & Umbrella Courtship
Pretty Plough Boy & Little Gypsey Lass
Queen Victoria
Queen of May & Colin & Phebe
Robin Hood & Tom Haulyard
Rambling Sailor & Tired Soldier
Ranting Parson & Gay old Man
Rest! Warriors Rest, Fly not Yet & Canadian Boat Song
Robin's Petition & Cold Winter is past
Rose of Allandale, Dr. Brown & Britannia
Some here to Roam—Kate of Kintore—The Soldier's Dream
Sorrowful Husband—Pretty Star of the Night—Poor Dog Tray
Shannon and Cheesepeake & Ship Carpenter
Soldier's Tear & Time Enough for that
Steam Arm & Blue Eyed Stranger
Sucking Pig 4to.
The Nightingale—Who are you?
The Thorn 4to.
Time to Remember the Poor & Flashy Back & Hungry Belly
Three Frightened Virgins
Tom Bowling, the Open Sea & Young Paris
Thorney Moor Woods & Plato's Advice
Tom Moody & Bloody Miller
The Mountebank and Devil & The Flea
Tobacco & The Model
Termagant Wife & Sarah Wilson
The Sea's My Home! & Far, Far at Sea
The Storm & Tom Philpot
Time Enough for that & Little Mary
Undaunted Mary & Gallant Hussar
Wednesbury Cocking 4to.
William & Harriet & Green Willow
Woodland Mary & Sir John Barley-corn
Wounded Hussar & Flower o' Dunblane
When and Where & Beauty the Pride of a Soldier
Will Watch & Rambling Soldier
We've Lived & Loved Together & Farewell to the Mountain's
William and Phyllis—Fair Phebe
Young William of the Man of War—Caroline of Edinboro' town

A general Assortment of Childrens Books, School Books, and Account Books, constantly on Sale at the Lowest Wholesale Prices.

S. W. RUSSELL, PRINTER, MOOR STREET, BIRMINGHAM.

About three-fifths of Russell's catalogue is a bewilderingly miscellaneous collection of sentimental, patriotic and modish songs, together with more or less topical pieces, often with marked local reference. The remaining two-fifths are reprintings of traditional songs. Not all broadside printers had a similar output, but the same elements feature in all their work. These sheets of course reflect the tastes and preoccupations of the popular audience for which they were intended. Sport, crime, work, the cost of living, and the quality of life all appear in broadsides. Many of these ballads were as short-lived as a copy of today's newspaper, but others took root and passed into oral tradition. *Young Henry the poacher,* is the story of six men tried at Warwick Assizes for poaching, and transported to Van Dieman's Land for fourteen years. This ballad may have been inspired by two big trials of poachers held at Warwick early in 1829. It circulated nationally, was frequently reprinted, and survived in oral tradition until this century. *Young Henry* shows that the creation of new songs in traditional style continued until relatively recently. It also illustrates how the printed word and oral tradition might complement each other. Certainly, printed broadsides helped traditional carols to survive. Wood of Birmingham, to take only two examples, issued *The moon shines bright* and *Dives and Lazarus.* In 1910 Cecil Sharp found Mrs Gentie Phillips singing the first in Birmingham. He noted that she was 'a native of Tysoe in Warwickshire where this and many other carols were sung every Christmas'. *Dives* was sung at Farnborough.

The traditional songs of Warwickshire have never been well documented. Only 31 Warwickshire items are included in a large volume of 413 songs collected by Cecil Sharp in various parts of the country. All too often, one finds only a reference: 'a few scraps of ancient carols at Wimpstone'; 'a Warwickshire carol *[The carnal and the crane]*, still sung'; 'in the public-houses [on Club Day at Tysoe] the old men were asked to sing the two folk-songs that still lingered.' More tantalisingly, writers quote only a verse or two. Even the excellent Bloom gives only two verses of *The cruel gardener* 'from an old lady, well over ninety', who knew the whole ballad, and two verses out of 27 of *Lord Thomas.* When a full text is quoted, the tune is generally not considered worthy of a mention. One must be grateful to find texts of Warwickshire versions of *I wish, I wish, The bitter withy* (from Bidford) and *The holly and the ivy.* Savage obtained the last from 'a jovial son of the soil ... the man supplying his own music, a melodian (*sic*):

> The holly and the ivy,
> We know it all does grow;
> Over all the trees that's in the wood,
> The holly bears the crown.
> *Chorus*
> O, the rising of the sun,
> The running of the deer,
> The playing of the merry band,
> Sweet singing in the choir.
>
> The holly bears a blossom
> As white as any snow;
> And Mary bore sweet Jesus
> To be our Saviour.
>
> The holly bears a prickle
> As sharp as any thorn;
> And Mary bore sweet Jesus
> On Christmas Day in the morn.
>
> The holly bears a berry
> As red as any blood;
> And Mary bore sweet Jesus
> To do poor sinners good.
>
> The holly bears a bark
> As bitter as any gall;
> And Mary bore sweat Jesus
> To die to save us all.

An alternative chorus, sung 'many years ago', is also given:

> O, the rising of the sun,
> The chasing of the deer;
> Shakespeare went to Charlecote Park
> At this merry time of year.

Young Henry the Poacher.

Come all you wild and wicked youths, wherever
   you may be,
I pray you give attention and listen unto me.
The fate of us poor Transports as you shall
   understand,
The hardships that we undergo upon Vad Dieman's land,

CHORUS.

Young men all now beware,
Lest you are drawn into a snare.

My parents rear'd me tenderly, good learning
   give to me,   my destany,
Till by bad company was beguil'd which prov'd
I was brought up in Warwickshire near South
   hamton did dwell,   known full well,
My name it is young Henry in Harbourn

Me and five more went out one night into
   Squire Dunhill's park,   it proved dark,
To see if we could get some game, the night
And to our great misfortune they trepanned us
   with speed.   our hearts to bleed,
And sent us off to Warwick Jail, which made

It was at the March Assizes to the bar we did
   repare.   sentence there,
Like Job we stood with patience, to hear our
There being some old offenders which made
   our case go hard,   sent on board,
My sentence was for fourteen years then I was

The ship it bore us from the land, the Speed-
   well was by name, (plough'd the raging main,
For full five months and upwards, boys, we,
Neither land nor harbour could we see believe
   it is no lie,   one blue sky,
All around us one black water, boys, above us

I often look behind me, towards my native
   Shore,   see no more.
That cottage of contentment, which we shall
Nor yet my own dear father who tore his hoary
   hair,   me bear,
Likewise my tender mother the womb that did

The fifteenth of September 'twas then we made
   the land,   hand-in-hand,
At four o'clock we went on shore, all chained
To see our fellow-sufferers we felt I cant tell
   how.   plough.
Some chained unto a harrow, and others to a

No shoes os stockings they had on, or hat had
   they to wear,   feet and hands bare
But a leathern frock and linsey drawers, their
They chained them up by two and two like
   horses in a teem.   lacky cane,
Their driver he stood over them with his Ma-

Then I was marched to Sidney town without
   any more delay,   keeper to be
Where a gentleman he bought me his hook
I took my occupation my master liked me well
My joys were out of measure and I'm sure no
   one can tell.

We had a female servant, Rossanna was her
   name   verhampton came
For fourteen years a convict was from Wol-
We often told our tales of love when we were
   blest at home,   eign lands to roam
But now we're rattling off our chains in for-

Jackson and Son, (late J. Russell,) Printers, 23

Moor-street, Birmingham.

Cecil Sharp's collecting in Warwickshire was not so extensive as one might have hoped. *The keeper* is perhaps the best-known song that he found in the county, though he doctored the words for publication, in deference to contemporary taste. Here are the original words, from Robert Kinchin of Ilmington:

O the keeper he a-shooting goes
And all amongst his bucks and does,
And O for a shoot at the barren doe
She's amongst the leaves of the green O.
Chorus
Jackie boy, Master,
Sing 'ee well?
Very well.
Hey down, ho down, derry derry down.
She's amongst the leaves of the green O
To my hey down down,
To my ho down down,
Hey down, ho down, derry derry down,
She's amongst the leaves of the green O

The first doe that he shot at he missed,
And the second doe he trimmed he kissed,
And the third ran away in a young man's breast,
She's amongst the leaves of the Green O.

The fourth doe then she crossed the plain,
The keeper fetched her back again,
O and he tickled her in a merry vein,
She's amongst the leaves of the green O.

The fifth doe she crossed the brook,
The keeper fetched her back with his long hook,
And what he done at her you must go and look,
For she's amongst the leaves of the green O.

It seems clear, then, that many ordinary people knew songs well enough to sing them, and were acquainted with others. Certain individuals acquired a special reputation. The Kenilworth grave-digger, Luke Sturley, sang at work to amuse himself, and in pubs to entertain others. His headstone stands by the west door of Kenilworth Church. Savage knew a wandering pedlar, like Autolycus, who came from Shipston and 'delighted the folk of the countryside for more than forty years. But alas! his wares and fiddle are now laid aside, although his original manuscript music and songs, in a somewhat altered form, survive, and amuse those who are vainly striving to re-introduce the old customs in their false, little-understood theatrical style'. Walter Tomlinson wrote in the 1880s of being able to find in Warwickshire, 'in any remote country village . . . some old man or other . . . whose head was a perfect storehouse and repository of these popular ballads'.

In the towns traditional music held its own alongside the music hall and variety-stage repertoire. Many street cries could be heard until relatively recently; perhaps 'Any old iron? Any scrap iron? Any rags or bones?' is the only one left. The ballad-sellers continued to hawk their wares. A *Birmingham Daily Gazette* reporter visited the Onion Fair in 1865: 'To his knowledge his pockets were searched more than once as he stood gazing at the dancers in front of the circus, looking at a lamb with ten legs, or reading the choice specimens of ballad literature – Hibernian most – pasted against the walls of St Martin's Church, Spiceal Street'. Twenty years later the *Birmingham Weekly Mercury* still pictured the street hawker and the ballad-singer with his 'yard of songs for one penny'.

A notice read, 'No larking or singing', but Cecilia Costello ignored it and sang with her workmates at the screw factory where she was employed in the 1890s. Here is one of her songs:

> Aye for Saturday night, Sunday is a-coming;
> I'll go up the town and meet my love a-coming.
> *Chorus*
> O for some rum, rum, rum, O for some gin and brandy;
> O for some rum, rum, rum, for my young man's a dandy.
>
> Aye for silver spoons, and aye for plates and dishes,
> Aye for the lad I love that broke my heart with kisses.
>
> I know who is sick, I know who is sorry;
> I know who I love, but I don't know who I'll marry.

As I lay in my bed the water from the ceiling
Fell in my love's eye and sent him off a-squealing.

As I lay in my bed, and you know who lay with me,
I know what I said, but you don't know what he give me.

Townspeople sometimes felt a pride in surroundings which others
might think grim:

Mary, Mary, Brummagem Mary, how does your allotment
   grow?
Yo've 'ad some shy knocks through werkin' at Kynoch's,
Although you don't mind, we all know.
Yo've never seen Arizona, and Texas is not your abode,
Yo're just Mary, Mary, Brummagem Mary, what lives up the
   Pairsher Road.

Summer Lane, a slum street in a tough area, had a reputation for
nicknames and prize-fighters. Mr Laurence Rogers, who was born
there in 1903, assures me that, some years after his marriage, one of
his workmates called at the house, asking for him: his wife said no-
one called Laurence lived there. The man tentatively mentioned
his nickname, 'Pummy', and Mrs Rogers immediately invited him
in, saying: 'Why didn't you say that in the first place?' Mr Rogers
was fond of singing, and he and his wife, sometimes joined by
friends and relatives, held sing-songs round the piano, which they
called 'cats' concerts'. Their repertoire was taken from popular songs
of the day, which they had heard at the Aston Hippodrome; the
words came from penny or twopenny song-sheets. Mr Rogers
knows one song about his own area, which he learned in about
1920. Like *Brummagem Mary* it rejects imported American culture,
in preference to 'a song about your own home town':

Now we've heard you singing of your Alabam,
And who's a-sighing 'bout your dad and your mam;
You say that you've heard your Tennessee Call,
Yet you never saw Tennessee at all,
And we are fed up with your Mississip,

Mary, Mary, Brummagem Mary

Mary, Mary, Brummagem Mary, how does your al- lotment grow?

Yo've 'ad some shy through workin' at Kynoch's, Al- though yo' dont mind we all know.
knocks

Yo've never seen Ari- zo- na, and Texas is not your a- bode, Yo're just

Mary, Mary, Brummagen Mary, what lives up the Pairsher Road.

Summer Lane

(Verse 2) Now if you've friends from the country for a day or two, You

take 'em round the town, the sights to view; First in Cut- ler's for a

drink you call, You show 'em the fountain and the Old Town Hall, Then a

long Colmore Row the car you catch To see the water melons on the

old black patch; But there's one sight you must not miss, Before your must say good- just
friends bye,

mention this: You want to see the palm trees swaying. —

way down Summer Lane, Every Satur- day night there's a

ju- bi- la- tion, Hear the birds a- singing in the Sa- lu- ta- tion;

Though there's snow in Snow Hill,. There's no cause to take a train To your

southern home where the weather is warm, It's always summer in Summer Lane.

They're changing dear old Brummagem

They're changing dear old Brummagem be - fore our very eyes,

Pla- ces that we know so well are hard to re - cog - nise; In

Balsall Heath and Lady- wood, in As - ton and Newtown, The

blocks of flats are going up, the homes are coming down.

The first time I met her

The first time I met her, I met her in white,

All in white, all in white, she gave me such a fright,

Down in the dark al - ley where no - bo - dy goes.

The Mason-Dixie line has given us all the pip;
Your songs from Yankee land have been done brown,
So let's have a song about your home town.
Chorus
You want to see the palm trees swaying, way down
     Summer Lane,
Every Saturday night there's a jubilation,
Hear the birds a-singing in the Salutation;
Though there's snow in Snow Hill,
There's no cause to take a train
To your southern home where the weather is warm —
It's always summer in Summer Lane.

Now if you've friends from the country for a day or two,
You take 'em round the town, the sights to view;
First in Cutlers for a drink you call,
You show 'em the fountain and the old Town hall,
Then along Colmore Row the car you catch
To see the water melons on the old black patch;
But there's one sight you must not miss,
Before your friends must say goodbye, just mention this.

Summer Lane is still there, though changed out of all recognition
after re-development. With it has gone a local identity, which
cannot easily be re-created on the sprawling housing estates:

They're changing dear old Brummagem before our very eyes,
Places that we knew so well are hard to recognise;
In Balsall Heath and Ladywood, in Aston and Newtown,
The block of flats are going up, the homes are coming down.
Chorus
Oh, the old folks miss their neighbours, the friendly doorstep
     chat,
Life is very different in a fourteenth story flat.
They've planned a bright new city without a single slum;
They call it redevelopment, but will it still be Brum?

Oh, the Bull Ring is so altered now you've really got to search
To find the only landmark left, St Martin's Parish Church.

They've cleared whole streets of tunnelbacks, destroyed a
  neighbourhood,
And shifted half the families right out to Chelmsley Wood.

In spite of these clearances, one aspect of traditional lore remained
strong. In primary school playgrounds the rhymes and chants
accompanying skipping and ball-bouncing, or just for sheer fun or
play with words, continue as they always did. The strength of the
tradition is illustrated by the many variants of classic children's
songs like *Rosy apple, On the mountain* and *The big ship sails*. Others
less well-known, are also traditional:

> The first time I met her, I met her in white,
> All in white, all in white, she gave me such a fright.
> *Chorus*
> Down in the dark alley where nobody goes.
>
> The next time I met her, I met her in pink,
> All in pink, all in pink, she gave off such a stink.
>
> The next time I met her I met her in brown,
> All in brown, all in brown, I pulled her knickers down.
>
> The next time I met her, I met her in green,
> All in green, all in green, she said the doctor's been.
>
> The next time I met her, I met her in blue,
> All in blue, all in blue, she said the doctor's due.
>
> The next time I met her, I met her in fawn,
> All in fawn, all in fawn, she said the baby's born.
>
> The next time I met her, I met her in red,
> All in red, all in red, she said the baby's dead.
>
> The next time I met her, I met her in check.
> All in check, all in check, I wrung her bloody neck.

—13—

The Everlasting
Circle

JANUARY

The custom of letting in the new year was popular in Warwickshire. 'On New Year's morning, as every one can sorrowfully testify', wrote J. A. Langford in 1875,

> no peace or rest is to be procured after twelve o'clock, till the dawn of day. Bands of noisy urchins knock at your door, and shout:
>
>> I wish you a merry Christmas and a happy new year,
>> A pocket full of money and a cellar full of beer,
>> A good fat pig to serve you all the year:
>> Open the door and let the New Year in,
>> Open the door and let me in.
>
> This must be said by boys or men, it being unlucky for the gentler sex to take part in these greetings.

A Birmingham woman, aged about 40, interviewed in 1966, described a similar procedure:

You have to have a man with . . . dark hair, and brown eyes, and you let him run in through the front door. He comes and he runs round the table, and he says:

A pocketful of money and a cellarful of beer,
And a big fat goose to last you all the year.

And he pokes the fire, runs three times round the table, shouts

New 'air [year] in, new 'air in

with the door open, and then runs out. . . . It was considered bad luck, you see, if you didn't let the new year in.

Sadly, she added: 'But the children don't know about it.'

At Coventry it was the custom to eat 'God Cakes' on New Year's Day. 'They are', runs a description written in 1856, 'of a triangular shape, of about half an inch thick, and filled with a kind of mince-meat. There are halfpenny ones cried through the street; but others of much greater price – even up to one pound – are used by the upper classes.' The modern equivalent of the God Cake is the 'Coventry', a jam pastry, but it is eaten on other days besides the first day of January.

Plough Monday, the first Monday after Twelfth Night, was celebrated at Tysoe until within living memory. At Ettington, until the late eighteenth century, a plough decorated with ribbons was drawn through the village and money collected. There was also a race between the farm girls and the plough boys.

FEBRUARY

Candlemas Day (2 February) marked, all being well, the last day of winter:

If Candlemas Day be fair and bright,
Winter will have another flight;
If Candlemas Day be wind and rain,
Winter is gone and won't come again.

On Orange Day (5 February) at Kineton, oranges were sold cheaply in the market square, until 1940. St Valentine's Day (14th) is still commemorated by the sending and receipt of Valentines. These can be signed or anonymous, and profess either love or dislike. At Tysoe, some children used to have the day off school, and at Armscot the boys went round singing for apples, which they fried in fritters. Their little chant was:

> Good morrow Valentine,
> First it's yours, then it's mine,
> Please give I a Valentine.

In *A Midsummer Night's Dream*, Shakespeare refers to the old belief that birds begin to mate on Valentine's Day. He seems to have known about a number of calendar customs. In *All's well that ends well*, he uses the expression, as 'fit . . . as a pancake for Shrove Tuesday'. At Alcester there is a ladies' pancake-race on Shrove Tuesdays, which was started seven years ago. The prize, usually a stainless-steel frying-pan, is presented by the Lord of the Manor, the Marquis of Hertford. Much rougher sports – like Atherstone street football – used to be played on this day, and Joseph Hill of Stratford mentions throwing at cocks. 'Very sharp frost', he noted on 5 February 1799; 'snow was so deep on the grownd that the boys could not find no other place to throw at cocks but on the ice on the river.' William Odell of Coventry, who died in 1884, could 'just remember the throwing at cocks on Shrove Tuesday in the Windmill Fields, and at Spon Wake'.

MARCH

Mothering Sunday, the fourth in Lent, normally falls in March. It was the custom in Warwickshire, until late in the nineteenth century, for grown-up children, both married and unmarried, to visit their mothers:

> The lad and lass on Mothering Day
> Hie home to their mother so dear;
> 'Tis a kiss for she and a kiss for they,
> A chine of pork and a sprig of bay.
> A song and dance – but never a tear.

While mother prepared the traditional meal of pork, the children took her little delicacies, like frumenty. Many shops stocked specially prepared wheat for the occasion. Frumenty (called 'furmatty' at Shipston) was made by putting wheat in a bag on the floor and beating it to separate the husk from the grain. The prepared wheat meant that this process could be omitted, for it was already de-husked. The grain was boiled with plums to make a pudding. By the early twentieth century the custom was in marked decline, though apprentices still made a point of getting home to see their parents and eating pork and frumenty. Today, cards — sometimes made and coloured at school — are sent to mothers, or flowers given.

APRIL

All Fools' Day (1 April) seems in little danger of dying out. Schoolchildren are no longer as learned as the boys at Rugby, who used to send first and second formers to the stocks to see Tom Nemo and Peter Nullus. But classic schoolboy tricks — books balanced on doors and drawing-pins on chairs — are still played on 1 April. Mother is invited to look at the results of imagined minor catastrophes like broken crockery — but only in the morning, for the jokes, according to tradition, must end at noon.

Easter, which normally falls during April, was surrounded by many customs and beliefs. If it fell earlier, and specifically on 25th March:

> When Easter falls on Lady Day's lap,
> Beware, old England, of a clap.

Easter Day was all-important and one wore something new to prevent bad luck. On Easter Monday the young men of Coleshill tried to catch a hare. If they could present it the parson before ten o'clock in the morning he had to give them a calf's head, a hundred eggs and a groat (fourpence). There was a similar custom at Wootton Wawen. A Birmingham song describes how:

> At Easter time girls fair and brown
> Used to come roly-poly down;
> And they showed their legs to half the town,
> The good old sights of Brummagem.

Newhall Hill was where they rolled down. Church clipping was also known in Birmingham:

When I was a child, as sure as Easter Monday came, I was taken to see the children clip the churches. This ceremony was performed, amid crowds of people and shouts of joy, by the children of the different charity-schools, who at a certain hour flocked together for the purpose. The first comers placed themselves hand in hand with their backs against the church [St Martin's], and were joined by their companions, who gradually increased in number, till at last the chain was of sufficient length completely to surround the sacred edifice. As soon as the hand of the last of the train had grasped that of the first, the party broke up, and walked in procession to the other church [St Philip's], (for in those days Birmingham boasted but of two), where the ceremony was repeated.

Church clipping continues in at least one part of the country, but it disappeared long ago in Birmingham.

Easter Monday and Tuesday were also heaving or lifting days. On Monday the men heaved the women, 'that is, took them up lengthwise in their arms, as a mother would her baby, and kissed them. All were served alike – the buxom, the slender, the comely, the plain, the saucy, and the shy'. On Tuesday the women retaliated. Heaving was widespread throughout the county, and rank was no protection; even the celebrated Dr Parr of Hatton was lifted by the girls. 'The women's day', wrote a Birmingham observer, 'was the most amusing':

Many a time have I passed along the streets inhabited by the lower orders of people, and seen parties of jolly matrons assembled round tables on which stood a foaming tankard of ale. There they sat in all the pride of absolute sovereignty, and woe the luckless man that dared to invade their prerogatives! As sure as he was seen he was pursued – as sure as he was pursued he was taken – and as sure as he was taken he was heaved and kissed, and compelled to pay sixpence for 'leave and licence' to depart.

A report from Birmingham in 1885 says that heaving 'was still kept up in some of the back streets of the town a few years back, and though it may have died out now with us, those who enjoy such amusements will find the old custom observed in villages not far away'. One of these was Avon Dassett in the south of the county; there were undoubtedly others.

At Coventry, bonfires were lit in the streets at Easter, and two weeks later, on Hock Tuesday, an ancient play was performed, which re-enacted the defeat of the Danes in 1002. These traditions disappeared long ago, but the Riding of St George (23 April) was preserved until recently. There is a tradition that the saint was born in Coventry, and on 23 April, a man representing him rode a horse through the town, accompanied by a woman, named Sabra, who led a captive dragon. A similar ride took place at Stratford, where the main festivities on St George's Day are now to celebrate Shakespeare's birthday.

MAY

On the eve and early morning of May Day, young men and women used to collect greenery and blossoms to decorate the houses of the village and its maypole. This is the practice to which Lysander refers in *A Midsummer Night's Dream*, when he mentions the 'wood, a league without the town', where he and Helena had previously met 'to do observance to a morn of May'. Such customs scandalised the puritans. The Coventry maypole was taken down in 1591, and was not restored until 1661. At Henley-in-Arden the May gatherings were stopped in 1655, when the Quarter Sessions dealt with 'unlawful meetings of vain and idle persons . . . , for erecting May Poles and May Bushes, and for using of Morris Dances and other heathenish and unlawful customs, the observation whereof tendeth to draw together a great concourse of loose people.' At about the same time, Thomas Hall, Curate of King's Norton, was publishing his compendiously-titled treatise, *The loathsomnesse of long hair, with an appendix against painting, spots, naked breasts, etc.* He followed this with a violent attack on the May celebrations, which took place on the village green. His *Funebria florae. or the downfall of the May-games* attacked 'ignorants, atheists, papists, drunkards, swearers, swashbucklers, maid-marians, morrice-dancers, maskers, mummers, May-pole stealers, health-drinkers, together with a rapscallion rout of fiddlers, fools, fighters, gamesters, lewd-women, light-women, contemners of magistracy, affronters of ministry, disobedient to parents, misspenders of time, and abusers of the creature, etc.' Parson Hall

was also the schoolmaster at the local grammar school, and the
building still stands in the churchyard. He even opposed the custom
of barring-out, which permitted the boys to arrive at school before
the master on a traditional day, and shut him out, so that they
would be given a day's holiday. Hall 'abhorred that lewd Custom
of Schollers shutting their Masters out of doores & having broke in
upon his boys severall yeares & drove them forth, at last (being too
venturous & building too much upon former success) He had one
tooth strucke out, & two crazed; but since the breaking of his teeth
broke the neck of Vile custome, it pleased him well.'

Dr Parr, Rector of Hatton, near Warwick, in the following
century, was a great supporter of popular traditions, even though he
was a 'literary gladiator, a prize-fighter in Greek and Latin', who
had crossed swords with Dr Johnson.

> 'Whilst he was arguing', Dr Parr says, 'I observed that he
> stamped; upon this, I stamped. Johnson said, "Why did you
> stamp, Dr Parr?" I replied, Because you stamped; and I was
> resolved not to give you the advantage even of a stamp in the
> argument.'

Parr, according to William Gardiner, was 'one of the few persons
bold enough to maintain his opinion of civil and religious liberty in
the frightful times of the Birmingham riots' in the early 1790s. In
church he always retired to the vestry to smoke a pipe during the
long anthem which invariably preceded his sermons. He used to
rebuke a late-comer publicly by saying, 'John, how many times do I
have to tell you not to stump up the aisle in those hob-nailed boots?'
William Hone wrote this of him:

> The late Dr Parr, the fascinating controverser, the skilful
> controverter, the first Greek scholar, and one of the greatest and
> influential men of the age, was a patron of May-day sports.
> Opposite his parsonage-house ... stood the parish Maypole,
> which in the annual festival was dressed with garlands,
> surrounded by a numerous band of villagers. The doctor was
> 'first of the throng', and danced with his parishioners the gayest
> of the gay. .... He always spoke of this festivity as one wherein
> he joined with peculiar delight to himself, and advantage to his
> neighbours. He was deemed eccentric, and so he was; for he was

never proud to the humble, nor humble to the proud. His eloquence and wit elevated humility, and crushed insolence; he was the champion of the oppressed, a foe to the oppressor, a friend to the friendless, and a brother to him who was ready to perish.

The Warwick celebrations used to include a booth for dancing in the Market Square, and processions with people dressed up to represent such worthies as Robin Hood, Little John and Sir Guy of Warwick.

Welford, near Stratford, is one of the few places in the country, and the only one in the county, where a permanent maypole still stands. Many villages had temporary ones, often made from birch trees which the local people acquired as best they could, hence Parson Hall's reference to 'May pole stealers'. At Wootton Wawen, 'About an hundred yards to the right hand of the bottom of the bridge stood a May Pole which I recollect being dressed in due form for several years, and a high holiday it was considered by the neighbouring population' — so wrote Sarah Chandler, who died in 1845 at the age of 89. Some sort of celebration continued at Knowle until 1914, when, like so many customs, it was ended by the Great War.

Within living memory, children went round with branches of greenery, decorated with ribbons and brightly coloured rags, collecting coppers from passers-by. At Alscot, children from the four villages on the estate collected flowers and made them into double-hooped garlands on long poles. The four garlands — one for each parish — were taken to the squire's house on May morning. When he and his family had heard the May songs, the singers were given cowslip wine and cakes. Then they went round all the farms with their garlands. Morley, writing in 1900, says that the general rule in 'Shakespeare's greenwood', by which he presumably means the area round Stratford, was to celebrate on Old May Day (12th). His account is worth quoting at length:

The earlier hours of the previous day are occupied by the children in a perambulation of the parish, calling upon the farm folk and other residents for gifts of flowers and finery with which to decorate their maypoles. In the evening the maypole is hoisted on the village green, or in some paddock or orchard lent for the purpose, and the election of the Queen takes place. Some villages have a King and Queen, but the majority elect a Queen only . . .

On the morrow the Queen and her attendants, as richly bedizened as flowers, ground ivy, May blossoms, and patchwork can make them, again parade the boundary of the parish, singing their May songs (first at the doors of the Squire and Parson, and then at the houses of the lesser people) round a portable maypole; finally returning to their ground or play-mead, where the songs are sung over again in the following words, to a generally recognised home-made tune.

'Tis always on the twelfth of May,
We meet and dress so gaily;
For tonight will merry be,
For tonight will merry be,
For tonight will merry be,
We'll sing and dance so gaily.

The sun is up and the morn is bright,
And the twelfth of May is our delight,
Then arouse thee, arouse, in the merry sweet light,
Take the pail and the labour away.

That dear little girl,
Who lives in yon sky,
With the lilies and the roses,
Shall never be forgot.

Yonder stands a lovely lady,
Who she is we do not know,
Who she is we do not know;
We will take her for her beauty
Whether she answers Yes or No.

Then shake the money-box about,
And call on every lady.
For tonight will merry be,
For tonight will merry be,
For tonight will merry be,
We'll sing and dance so gaily.

When the songs had been sung at the end of the day, there is dancing in the evening. Some villages, like Charlecote, Bidford, Temple Grafton, Hillborough and Long Compton ... can conclude at the Rectory.

At Shipston, Tredington and Stratford, the chimneysweeps went the rounds, carrying garlands. At Coventry they had a Jack-in-the-green.

Their maypole, as we used to call it, was a large cylinder of greenery, eight or ten feet in height, and probably as much in diameter. It was lightly built, so that a man could walk inside it. In front was a small peephole, covered with muslin, with a fancy rosette at each corner, and the whole structure was decorated with bows and ends of bright local ribbons. Half-a-dozen sweeps, some dressed as females, would caper round Jack to the music of a fiddle. They carried long wooden spoons to collect from the bystanders, and the occasional pauses for light refreshment made the steps of the dance grow more and more uncertain as the day progressed. The fiddler played one particular tune – a country jig of three phrases.

In some places – at Bidford and Ilmington, for instance – the morris dancers would come out on May Day, as they did on Whit Sunday.

After the Restoration, some of the First of May celebrations were transferred to 29 May, the day when Charles II made his triumphal entry into London. This was variously Oak Apple, Oak Ball, or Oak Leaf Day, for, although Charles hid in the oak tree on 4 September, the two occasions were telescoped in popular tradition. There is a Warwickshire story that he had a pigeon with him in the tree and when the roundheads appeared, he released it. This made them think there was no-one in the tree, otherwise, they reasoned, the bird would have flown earlier.

Local carters, even in Birmingham, usually decorated their horses' heads as well as their own hats with oak sprigs on 29 May. Houses displayed oak boughs, leaves, or apples, and oak balls were worn in hats or button holes. Old soldiers in the Leycester Hospital at Warwick preserve this custom, though it seems to have died out in the rest of the county. Children wore oak leaves too. If they forgot, their friends stung their legs with nettles; after 12 noon this did not apply. The church bells were rung on the 29th, another custom which has disappeared. The last villages to observe this were Hampton and Middleton.

Seagulls used to be fairly rare in the land-locked county of Warwickshire. If schoolboys at Oakfield, Rugby, could spot a flight of them in May — and a flight meant two or more — they might claim a half day's holiday.

The moveable feast of Whitsun normally falls in May. On Whitsun Eve until the 1870s farmers at Tanworth-in-Arden used to give the whole of their milk-yield to their neighbours. Sarah Chandler remembered the custom at Wootton Wawen nearly a century earlier:

> The 25th May 1760 was Whitsunday. On that morning my usual attendant came ... (to) take me to the hall window to see my Father distribute the Milk. It was a good old custom at that time in the parish of Wootton for the poor women to go to the farm houses on the morning of Whitsunday and milk the Cows; and the Milk was then divided amongst them; and every poor family indulged in a luxury on that day named *Frumentary*, something like rice Milk, only that it was made with baked wheat instead of rice, and when properly palated with sugar and spice was a very nice article.

JUNE

Ascension Day, which comes forty days after Easter, often falls in June. On Ascension morning the choir of Wroxall Abbey School sing hymns from the tower of the parish church. It was the practice, earlier this century, to hold services on the top of St Mary's tower at Warwick, but now choirs sing hymns from different towers in succession at 6 a.m.

The preceding week is Rogation Week, when many towns and villages used to beat the bounds. The clergy, wardens, and principal inhabitants toured the parish boundaries. Bread and ale were provided by the parish, and small boys were bumped, beaten or dipped, to impress the local topography on their minds. In some places a broad red arrow was painted on boundary marks. The procession stopped from time to time to hear the parson read aloud from the Gospels. Normally this was done under the shade of an oak tree, and some of these trees are called Gospel Oaks to this day: there is one at Snitterfield, for example. Another, in Birmingham, no longer exists, but it has given its name to an area of the city. Stratford, Kenilworth, and Leek Wootton all observed beating the bounds at Rogationtide, though others preferred a different season.

St Barnabas' Day falls on the 11th June, and there was a saying, 'Barnaby bright, Barnaby light, Longest day, Shortest night', though the rhyme more properly applies to 21st June since the change of calendar in 1752. On Midsummer Eve (23rd) fires were lit in the streets of Coventry and Warwick, but this custom only survived until the sixteenth century. Coventry provided feasting, drinking, and a procession of giant figures made of wicker-work. As in May, the houses were decorated with flowers and birch boughs.

At midnight on Midsummer Eve, girls might see their future husbands by scattering fern-seed and saying:

Fern seed I sow, fern seed I hoe,
In hopes my true love will come after me and mow.

Trinity Week, another movable date, often falls in June, and was the occasion of the great Coventry Show Fair.

JULY

Mabel Ashby describes Tysoe Club Day, the local sick and provident society feast, which took place annually in July:

On the Saturday preceding the Sunday of the church's patronal festival, two or three booths were set up in the street, selling gingerbread to the children. These were the last crumbs of the old fun fair on the green. In the public-houses the old men were asked to sing the two folk-songs that still lingered, and on the Sunday morning a special sermon was preached in church: after that, at Sunday dinner, spiced raisin pudding was eaten in every house. Possibly the whole festival, service and pudding and song, went back via the medieval village guild and the founding of the village church to a pagan midsummer feast. Certain it is that the festival was felt to be the whole village's affair ... It was for this week that Tysoe men and women came back from the towns to see this old place and the home folk.

AUGUST

The freemen of Coventry — those who had served a seven-year apprenticeship in the town — had the right of keeping cattle on the common lands from Lammas (1 August) to Candlemas (2 February). The common land at Coventry was not fully enclosed until 1860, and up to that date there was an annual riding, held on Old Lammas Day (13 August): 'Every year on the thirteenth of August, it was the custom of the chamberlains, pinners, and such of the freemen as cared to join them, all mounted on horseback, to assert their rights by riding over the lands. Any gates or obstructions to free access were unceremoniously broken down'.

SEPTEMBER

Michaelmas Day (29 September) marked the end of the farming year and the beginning of the mop season. 'In the Vale of the Red Horse somewhere about Michaelmas Day sundry farm waggons may be seen at intervals piled high with articles of domestic furniture with the rustic children seated upon the top. These are the belongings of the hired labourer whose term of service being ended at one farm is removing to another. If the peasant walking at the horse's head be questioned as to his journey at so early an hour in the morning he will say, 'We be rimmin' to Tysoe, sir. Our turn's done at Radway, un' we'm obliged to get off on the ground afore the dag's [dew] dry'. Thus Morley, writing in 1900. Birmingham Onion Fair was held in this month.

OCTOBER

Mops, Runaway Mops and fairs continued. Candle auctions used to be held at the beginning of the month, at Warton, near Polesworth. The letting of roadside grazing rights was involved, and 'the bidding for each lot commenced with the lighting of a bit of candle about a quarter of an inch long. He who was last in when the light went out became the purchaser.' At one time the prices of hay, fodder and corn used to be proclaimed at the Warwick Quarter Sessions during Michaelmas Term. Schoolboys, as well as lawyers, have such a term, and at Warwick School by ancient tradition the Town Crier calls 'to bring a message from the Mayor of Warwick asking the Headmaster to grant the school a half holiday. This half holiday is always granted and nowadays is absorbed into our Michaelmas Term half-term break':

He comes with tricorn hat and red coat and arrives at my house at a time arranged. At that time the 950 boys of the school are gathered together in the Chapel quadrangle about a hundred yards away. The Senior Prefect collects the Town Crier and takes him to the boys, when the official part of his visit really begins. The words used thereafter are traditional. The Town Crier asks 'whoever is chief among you' to take him to the Headmaster's lodging. He makes this request at the end of a formal statement of greetings from the Mayor and Councillors of Warwick to the school and explains in that statement that he has been sent to ask for the half holiday. The Senior Prefect brings him to my study, the request is granted, the Town Crier returns to the boys and his statement of the half holiday is received with cheers, which are followed by cheers for the Mayor and Councillors of Warwick. All this takes about ten minutes. The boys then dismiss to their lessons and the Town Crier is taken round the school by the Senior Prefect and his deputy. The result of his visit to each classroom is that he returns about half an hour later to my study with his tricorn hat filled with coins, and just occasionally he needs a reserve container.

So writes the present headmaster, Mr Pat Martin.

In Warwick the beating of the bounds of the parish of St Mary's used to be in October, with schoolboys – presumably not from Warwick School – ceremonially beaten to help their memories.

At Hallowe'en (31st October) a form of divination took place, certainly at Knowle, and perhaps elsewhere. After a game of apple-bobbing, the winner of an apple peeled it in one long ribbon, and threw it over his left shoulder. On landing it was supposed to form the initials of one's future wife (or husband). Modern Hallowe'en parties still sometimes have apple-bobbing, and often turnip lanterns.

NOVEMBER

All Saints' Day is the first, and All Souls' Day, the second of November. Souling took place not on All Souls' Day, as might be expected, but on its eve, All Saints' Day. People went round the houses and farms, singing songs, and collecting food or money. Special soul cakes were baked. In Warwickshire, seed cakes were popular. Shakespeare mentions souling in *The Two Gentlemen of Verona*, but the custom seems to have died relatively early in Warwickshire.

This Bonfire Night rhyme was used at Long Marston:

> Please to remember the fifth of November.
> Gunpowder plot
> Shall never be forgot
> As long as old England is tied in a knot.
> A stick and a stake
> For King George's sake,
> Will you please to give us a faggot?
> If you won't give one we'll steal two
> The better for we and the worse for you.

The last two lines are very much applicable to small boys today, not only on 5 November, but many weeks before. They make their 'guy' from old clothes stuffed with straw or rags and wheel him in an old perambulator, asking passers-by to give them money. They also collect large quantities of wood – discarded furniture, sticks, tree branches, packing cases – for their bonfires; some of them are communal affairs, held on waste land, or even in the streets.

On St Martin's Day (11th) an ancient ceremony takes place before daybreak at Knightlow Hill. The steward of the Duke of Buccleuch stands beside a stone – all that remains of Knightlow Cross – and asks the assembled representatives of the villages in the hundred to pay their dues, called Wroth Silver. The men come forward and make their payment, which may originally have been in lieu of military service. The fine for default is twenty shillings for every penny [£1.00 for every ½p], or a white bull with red ears. After the ceremony, all concerned visit the Dun Cow Inn at Dunchurch for hot rum and milk. In 1976 Wroth Silver will be collected for the 786th time.

It was believed, at Shipston and elsewhere, that the quarter in which the wind lay at midnight on St Clement's Day (23rd) would indicate the direction of the prevailing wind until Candlemas (2 February). On St Clement's Day parties of children went round 'soliciting goodies and pence', and chanting a variety of rhymes. Here is one:

Clemeny, Clemeny, Clemeny mine!
A good red apple and a pint of wine.
Some of your mutton and some of your veal,
If it is good, pray give a deal;
If it is not, pray give some salt—
Butler, butler, fill in your bowl.
If thou fill'st it of the best,
The Lord'll send your soul to rest;
If thou fill'st it of the small,
Down goes butler, bowl and all.
Pray, good mistress, send to me,
One for Peter, one for Paul,
One for Him who made us all,
Apple, pear, plum, or cherry,
Any good thing to make us merry;
A browning buck, or a velvet chair.
Clement comes but once a year;
Off with the pot, and on with the pan,
A good red apple and I'll begin.

The barring-out at King Edward's School, Birmingham, used to take place on 26 November. There was another famous barring-out at Nuneaton Grammar School.

DECEMBER

At Stoneleigh, Duchess Dudley's charities provided doles of meat and coal for the poor on St Thomas's Day (21st). On the same day the poor throughout the county went 'a-gooding', 'a-corning' or 'a-Thomasing', as the custom was variously called. Basically, this was collecting any sort of provisions against the coming winter, and Christmas:

A Christmas gambol oft can cheer
The poor man's heart through half the year.

In some districts people specifically asked for corn (hence 'a-corning') to make frumenty. One of the many recipes for this dish says it should be made with baked wheat, sugar and dried currants, boiled in milk and thickened with flour and eggs. One of the St Thomas chants was:

> Little Cock Robin sat on a wall,
> We wish a merry Christmas,
> And a great snowfall;
> Apples to eat
> And nuts to crack
> We wish you a merry Christmas
> With a rap, tap, tap.

There was a widespread belief in Warwickshire that the farm animals knelt on Christmas Eve at midnight in adoration of the Christ Child. It was also customary at the same time to go down the garden to the beehives 'to hear the bees sing their Christmas carols'. This practice did not die out until within living memory. At Aston Hall there was a unique ceremony after supper on Christmas Eve. A table was brought out and on it were placed a brown loaf with twenty silver threepenny-bits on top, a tankard of ale, and pipes of tobacco. The two oldest servants sat by the table, to act as judges. The rest of the servants were then brought in by the steward, one at a time, covered by a sheet. The judges had to guess who they were from their shape, and a hand stretched out beyond the sheet to touch the loaf. The judges were allowed three guesses, and if they were right, the person was led away empty-handed. Otherwise he or she received a silver coin. 'When the money is gone the servants have full liberty to drink, dance, sing, and go to bed when they please.' Thus the *Gentleman's Magazine*, in 1795.

Sarah Chandler remembered Christmas in 1759. 'Beginning with Christmas Eve in the year 1759 (my third year), I perfectly remember on that day being carried by Thomas, an old Man-servant, to my Grandmother's — living in the Village of Wootton Wawen ... The object of my visit on that particular day was to see the Yule Block drawn to the house by a Horse, as a foundation for the Fire on Christmas Day, and according to the superstition of those times for the twelve days following, as the said Block was not to be entirely reduc'd to ashes till that time had passed by.'

Presumably, something would have been saved from the Yule log, until the next year:

Kindle the Christmas brand and then

Till sunrise, let it burn;
When quenched, then lay it up again
Till Christmas next return.
Part must be kept
Wherewith to tend
The Christmas log next year;
And when 'tis safely kept, the fiend
Can do no mischief here.

While old Thomas was drinking Sarah's health in Stingo, 'Carrol singers were heared at the Door. On its being opened, two tall Women entered, bearing between them a large Wassal Bowl, finely dress'd on the outside with Holly, Misseltoe, Ribbons, Laurustinus, and what other flowers could be had at that season. But what most delighted me was a pretty silver Cup with a handle on each side slung in the middle withinside, and moved about as it was carried round. They sang a long Carrol, with a chorus after each verse, repeating the word *Mirth, etc* which I could not understand, and I well remember I was sadly puzzled to know the meaning, and ask'd my poor brother when I return'd home, who imediately sang the whole of it to me, explaining this great difficulty, and asking me why I did not enquire of Grandma or old Thomas'. Sadly, she does not quote the 'carrol'.

To ensure good luck for the year, carol singers should ideally be let in at the front door and out at the back. Today, as a rule, they are not let in at all. They arrive outside, begin singing, and ring the doorbell after a few verses. Apart from carol-singers privately organized in small groups for their own benefit, organisations like schools and churches arrange larger events.

Wassailing continued in Warwickshire, particularly in the deep south of the county, till earlier this century. The drink in the bowl – and it has been suggested that the 'gossip's bowl' mentioned in *A Midsummer Night's Dream* was a wassail bowl – was made of ale, nutmeg, ginger, toast, and roasted crabs or apples. It was sometimes known as 'lamb's wool'. Savage writes: 'The people ... would wend their way by the light from a candle placed inside an improvised lantern, usually a swede, carved in the shape of a man's face, to the farm houses, and after knocking on the door would enter in, singing the following wassail carol':

Wisselton, wasselton, who lives here?
We've come to taste yer Christmas beer.
Up thu kitchen and down thu hall,
A peck of apples ull serve us all.
Holly and ivy and mistletoe;
Give us some apples and let us goo;
Up with yer stocking, on of yer shoe,
If yer ant got any apples mony ull do.
My carol's done, and I must be gone,
No longer can I stay here.
God bless you all, both great and small,
And send yer a happy new year'.

Notes

ABBREVIATIONS
NQ *Notes and Queries*
FL *Folklore*
FLJ *Folklore Journal*

Introduction, pages 11-13
115 BOOKS: R. E. Wilson, 'A hand-list of books relating to the
county of Warwickshire', *Transactions of the Archaeological Section
of the Birmingham and Midland Institute,* vol 71, 1955, 64ff.
J. H. BLOOM: for an account of his life (1860-1944) see U. Bloom,
The elegant Edwardian, 1957.
A. H. WALLS: quoted in W. Andrews, *Bygone Warwickshire,* 1893,
243-4.

1 *The heart of England,* pages 14-23
DRAYTON: *Polyolbion* XIII 2.
DIALECT: J. R. Wise in *Shakespeare: his birthplace and its
neighbourhood,* 1861, 149ff, lists 57 words still current which had
been used by Shakespeare. Those quoted are from *Hamlet* V i

(loggatts), *Merry Wives* I i (shovel board), *Titus* IV iv (honey stalks), *Anthony* III viii (brize), *Othello* V i (quat), *As you like it* II iv (batlet), and both *Hamlet* III i and *Winter's Tale* IV iii and V ii (fardel).

SHAKESPEARE AND FOLKLORE: see T. F. Thistleton Dyer, *Folk lore of Shakespeare*, 1883, F. Savage, *The flora and folk-lore of Shakespeare*, 1923, and H. N. Ellacombe, *The plant-lore and garden-craft of Shakespeare*, 1878.

SHAKESPEARE TRADITIONS: J. Burman, *In the forest of Arden*, 1948, 29 (at Aston Cantlow), Wise, 81 (at Radbrook).

HIS POACHING: C. G. Harper, *Summer days in Shakespeare land*, 1912, 115; J. Byng, *The Torrington diaries*, 1934-8, vol 1, 51-2, This account was written in 1781. Byng adds: 'This curiosity, taken from my manuscript, Mr M[alone] intends to insert in his new edition of Shakespeare'. Edward Malone duly inserted the item, but claimed that it was a forgery (see his edition of Shakespeare, 1821, vol 2, 144). For the argument that Shallow was in fact Gardiner, see L. Hotson, *Shakespeare versus Shallow*, 1931. The mention of the scene cut out of the play edition is in Harper, 123.

SHAKESPEARE'S CRAB: this is shown on Sheet 54 of the first O.S. 1″ map, published in 1831, from surveys done in 1811-15 (reprinted as Sheet 51 by David and Charles, 1970). The tree died, and was taken down in 1824, shortly after C. F. Green had sketched it. His picture is included, together with others of the Shakespeare villages, in his book, *The legend of Shakespeare's Crab-tree*, 1857, facing p.9. Green reported that the story of the crab-tree was very strong in oral tradition at the time. According to the *Gentleman's Magazine* 1794, vol 64, pt 2, 1062, the story had long been known in Warwickshire.

SHAKESPEARE VILLAGES: see Green, *passim;* Evesham NQ I, 177 (Friday Street).

PALMER'S PIECE: Harper, 153 (drowning version), V. Bird, *Warwickshire*, 1973, 60 (poisoning), Savage, 205. The field is by Cranhill Corner on the A439, half a mile from Hillborough Lane.

OTHER ANNE: V. Bird, 60, despite Harper's report (p. 154) that the ghosts 'have ceased to walk'.

SUTTON FOR MUTTON: NQ, 5 Ser., III, 145. The 'Bandylegs' and 'Yenton' variants are from G. F. Northall, *English Folk-Rhymes,*

1892, 78, and 'knock-knees' from W. Showell, *Dictionary of Birmingham*, 1885, 78.

DAFT DORSINGTON: Harper, 147.

SILHILL ON THE HILL: S. J. Coleman, *Warwickshire folklore*, 1952, 2.

DIRTY GRITTON: Savage, 203.

THERE'S BITERSCOTE: Coleman, *ibid.*

IDLICOTE ON THE HILL: Coleman, *ibid.*

CLIFTON: Thistleton Dyer, 157. There is a similar rhyme about Congleton in Cheshire, which is said to date from 1601.

THE ARMSCOT BOYS: J. H. Bloom, *Folk lore, old customs and superstitions in Shakespeare land*, 1930, 131.

PLACE PHRASES: G. F. Northall, *Folk phrases of four counties*, 1894, 16, 19 (Harborne and Henley), Northall, *Rhymes*, 164 (Coventry blue).

CIVIL WAR STORIES: V. Bird, 142-3 (General Ireton), H. Bett, *English myths and traditions*, 1952, 704 (Cromwell at Burton Dassett), F. W. Hackwood, *Olden Warwickshire: its history, lore and legend*, 1921, ch. 15, *passim* (spectral battle), T. Kemp, *A history of Warwick and its people*, 1905, 39-40 (Jeremiah Stone), Bloom, 99 (modern version), Showell, 284, (Erdington blacksmith), A. Mee, *Warwickshire*, 1966, 142-3 (Charles in the kitchen), Wise, 67 (King's Lane), *Birmingham Evening Mail*, 31.10.1974, p. 16 (headless ghost), and Mr Tom Langley of Birmingham (born 1907), interviewed by Roy Palmer, 1973 (the ghostly scream). Mr Langley's story is not mentioned in *A true relation of the inhumane cruelties exercised by the Cavaliers at Birmingham, Warwickshire*, 1643, quoted by R. K. Dent, *Old and new Birmingham*, 1878-80, vol 1, 42, and I have not seen it in print.

2 *A local habitation*, pages 24-32

ARISTOCRATIC ASSOCIATIONS: Mee, 180 (Ethelbald), V. Bird, 121 and 132-3 (Piers Gaveston), *ibid*, 192 (Henry Grey).

WARWICKSHIRE DIGGERS: J. C. Adams, *Hampton-in-Arden*, n.d., 12 (Hampton Field), E. F. Gay, 'The Midland revolt and the inquisitions of depopulation of 1607', in *Transactions of the Royal Historical Society*, XVIII, 1904, 216-7 (Captain Pouch). The quotations are from the proclamation of the Warwickshire diggers, printed in J. O. Halliwell, *The marriage of wit and wisdom*, 1846, 140-1.

RED HORSE: W. Dugdale, *The Antiquities of Warwickshire*, 1765, 392 (first edition, 1656), G. Miller, *Rambles round the Edge Hills and in the Vale of the Red Horse*, 1967, 5-6.

PUBLIC HOUSE TRADITIONS: A. Burgess, *Warwickshire*, 1950, 37 (Four Crosses), Savage, 320 (Four Alls), J. H. Drew, *Kenilworth*, 1971, 177 (Roebuck).

HIGHWAYMEN: V. Bird, 99-100 (Mitchell), Miller, 83-4 (the highwayman whose treasure was buried at Fenny Compton), E. Wootton, *The history of Knowle*, 1972, 60 (underground stable), Drew, *ibid*, 57 (the robber of Mr Leigh), Wootton, *ibid*, (Knowle robbery), P. Lavery, *Warwickshire in 1790*, 1974, 23 (the John Smiths), Harper, 281 (Stoneleigh gibbet), M. H. Bloxam, *Rugby, the school and neighbourhood; history and legends of Rugby and the neighbourhood*, 1889, 196 (the murder of William Banbury), Hackwood, *Olden*, 124 (Chester Road robbery), V. Bird, 24 (Gallows Hill Farm).

MORE CRIMES: Mee, 238 (death of Lady Dorothy), Bett, 77, and J. Burman, *Old Warwickshire families and their houses*, 1934, 30 (alleged crime of Sir Thomas Holte), NQ, 5 Ser., III, 145 (Moulden's Bridge), Wootton, 120 (Knowle stocks), Bloxam, 159 (Rugby stocks), Burman, *Arden*, 85 (Berkswell stocks).

LOCAL FEATURES: Coleman, 1 (Stockton stone), *ibid*, 2 (village knocked down by Cromwell), Dugdale, 44 (Churl's Piece), Coleman, 3 (Child's Oak), F. W. Bennett, *Tiddyoody pie*, 1930, 60 (St George's Elm), Savage, 171 (Bowshot Wood), W. H. Hutton, *Highways and byways in Shakespeare's country*, 1914, 208, and G. Morley, *Shakespeare's greenwood: the customs of the county*, 1900, 89 (Hiron's Hole).

BROOKS AND WELLS: F. W. Hackwood, *Warwickshire lore*, 1918-25, 16, (Allesley, Atherstone and Sketchley), F. B. Burbidge, *Old Coventry and Lady Godiva*, 1952, 67 (Allesley), Bloxam, 147 (Dunchurch), Burbidge, 64-5 (Hob's Hole).

ALCOCK'S ARBOUR: Dugdale, quoted in Bloom, 109-110.

YEBBERTON STORIES: Bennett, 33.

SONG: collated from elements in J. H. Bird, *Sam Bennett, the Ilmington fiddler*, 1952, 30-1, and Bloom, 130-1.

3 *Saints and sinners*, pages 33-44

SAINTS: V. Bird, 102-3 (St Nicholas at Willoughby), J. Burman, *Families*, 69-70, and Dugdale, 581 (St Augustine), Hackwood, *Olden*, 2-3 (St Edith).

MIRACLES: Dugdale, 450 (Sir Hugh), Bett, 68, W. H. Hutton, 317, FL, 1908, vol 19, 458-9 (Alice Croft).

CHURCH SITES: Wootton, 120 (Knowle), Hackwood, *Olden*, ch 1 (Warmington).

CHURCH TRADITIONS: Mee, 118 (Honiley), Burgess, 24 (Offchurch), F. W. Hackwood, *A collection of newspaper cuttings relating to Warwickshire*, 1903-16, 83 (Civil War executions), Dugdale, 451 (Devil's Door at Wroxall), V. Bird, 140-1, and Dugdale, 686 (Nicholas Broome), V. Bird, 138 (Richard Beauchamp), Mee. 206-7 (Henry Pudsey), *ibid*, 238 (inscription at Wolverton).

CHURCH MUSIC: Mee, 221 (angel instrumentalists), Adams, 87 (Hampton band), Bloom, 116 (bells) J. H. Bird, 22 (Barcheston rhyme), A. R. Wright and T. E. Lones, *British calendar customs: England*, 1938-40, vol 1, 15 (Shrove Tuesday bells), G. F. Northall, *A Warwickshire word-book*, 1896, 167 under 'Pancake bell', Wright, vol 1, 151 (Bonfire bells), *ibid*, vol 1, 144 (All Souls' Day bells at Solihull), *ibid*, vol 1, 207-8, and Bloom, 127 (Thomasing bell), R. Palmer, *Room for company*, 1971, 20-1 (bell wake song), Bett, 126-7 (Curdworth story), Bett, 129, and Hackwood, *Lore*, 16 (Whitnash).

THE INATTENTIVE AT SERMONS: Coleman, 17, and M. H. Powis, *Warwickshire's wealth of fancies*, 1943-4, article for 18.XII.44.

EPITAPHS: J. Aubrey, *Brief lives*, ed. O. L. Dick, 1965, 334 (John Combe), V. Bird, 26 (Richard Davies), *ibid*, 182 (Mott and Lewis), Mee, 60 (woodcutter), Showell, 136 (John Dowler), M. K. Ashby, *Joseph Ashby of Tysoe*, 1961 138 ('This life is a city . . . '; see also Showell, 136), Hackwood, *Olden*, 89 ('Man, it behoves . . . '), Burman, *Families*, 67, (John Randal), V. Bird, 186-7 "When Madness fires . . . ').

MARY ASHFORD: Showell, 11-13, Dent, 373-9, J. Jaffray, *Hints for a history of Birmingham*, 1855-6, ch. 35, 56-7, Hackwood, *Olden*, ch. 21, *passim*. The incident at Gosford Green is in *Richard II* I iii.

DIGGUM UPPERS: Tom Langley, *The Tipton Slasher*, Tipton, 1970, 20-1.

4 *God send Sunday*, pages 45-57
TITLE: NQ, 12, Ser. VII, 507 (Newbold) 'Come day, go day, God send pay day' or 'Sunday'.
PLOUGH MONDAY: Hackwood, *Olden*, 6-7, Powis, 18.XII,44.
HORSES: J. A. Langford, 'Warwickshire folklore and superstitions', in *Transactions of the Archaeological Section of the Birmingham and Midland Institute*, 1878, 22 (rhyme), Bloom, 82 (vocabulary).
PLANTING CROPS: Savage, 326, and Bloom, 82 (bean planting), Powis, 18.XII.44 (Whipped Cat; she is at variance with Bloom, who merely says that the feast is 'known as the "whipt cat"', p. 82), J. Purser, *Our Ilmington*, 1966, 29 (corn planting), J. Arch, *The story of his life*, 1898, ch. 2, and Ashby, 24 (bird scaring), NQ, 12 Ser., V, 160 ('Ye pigeons ... '), Savage, 326 ('Shoo-hoo ...'), Northall, *Rhymes*, 384, ('Cooo-oo ... '; see also *Birmingham Weekly Post* NQ, Oct-Nov. 1881, and – with music examples – R. Palmer, *The painful plough*, 1972, 9-10).
LAMBING:NQ 12 Ser., V, 160, Bloom, 89.
SHEEP SHEARING: *Winter's Tale*, IV iii, NQ, 12 Ser., IV, 155.
HAY HARVEST: Bloom, 84, Powis, 18.XII.44, Purser, 32-3, quoting a song entitled *Turmot hoeing*.
HARVEST: Savage, 336-7 (tithes), Powis, 11.XII.44, Savage, 336-7, Bennett, 67, Bloom, 116, P. Horn, *The Victorian country child*, Kineton, 1974, 79, quoting Joseph Ashby (gleaning), Ashby, 24 ('Though the disinherited ...').
HARVEST HOME: Savage, 338-9 (Binton), Bennett, 68 (ribbons), Bloom, 86 (driver) and 85 (rhymes, from Wimpstone), Savage, 339 (Marston rhyme), Morley, 121-2 (procession), Bennett, 69 ('flay'), J. Brand, *Observations on the popular antiquities of Great Britain*, 1849, vol 2, 27, Thistleton Dyer, 302, and *The Two Gentlemen of Verona* I i ('boots'), V. Bird, 186 (Wolvey), Bloom, 86, and Savage, 339 (health), J. H. Bird, 27-8 (motto), Bennett, 69, Savage, 333-4, and Wise, 100-1 (songs), Savage, 339 (Ragley), Wright, vol 1, 183 (last harvest home; the place is unfortunately not specified).
VARIOUS TRADES: the Bevington labourers' song was communicated to Roy Palmer by Miss. J. D. Webb of Evesham, a grand-daughter of the employer mentioned. It has been published in the *Evesham Journal* (26.7.1957). Purser, 24-5 (stone-breaker), Northall, *Rhymes*, 308-9 ('I'm a navvy').

MINERS: *Pit-talk, a survey of terms used by miners in the South Midlands,* Vaughan Papers in Adult Education, No. 15, University of Leicester, n.d. *passim* (vocabulary), R. Palmer, *Songs of the Midlands,* 1972, 94 (*The old miner;* the composer originated in Durham, but it was his experiences at Haunchwood Pit, Nuneaton, which caused him to write the song), V. Bird, 144 (brass at Baxterley Church).

INITIATIONS: J. Gutteridge, *Lights and shadows in the life of an artisan,* 1969 (orig. 1893), 98 (factory), Drew, 149 (choirboys), R. Crompton-Rhodes, *A Birmingham glossary,* unpublished typescript in Birmingham Reference Library (Outcome).

SAINT MONDAY: report quoted in E. R. Pike, *Human documents of the Victorian golden age,* 1966, 88.

MUSIC: Palmer, *Songs,* 91 ('When you get up'), R. Palmer, *A touch on the times,* 1974, 142-4 (washing and fuddling), Bloom, 53 (rough music).

COUNTRY WASH: Powis, 11.XI.44, Bloom, 40.

5 Sneeze on Monday, pages 58-70

PHRASES: Bennett, 13 and 44, Bloom, 132, NQ, 12 Ser., VI, 67, Northall, *Phrases* and *Word-book, passim,* Wise, 153.

LUCK: Wootton, 121-2, Bennett, 84-6, W. Andrews, *Bygone Warwickshire,* 246, Coleman, 12, Langford, 11-12, Morley, 63.

BIRDS: Andrews, 216, Powis, 8.I.45 and 29.I.45, Langford, 13, *Hamlet* II I ii (handsaw), Morley, 96, Douce, quoted in Langford, 23 (owl story).

WEATHER: Powis. 29;I;45 and 30.X.43, S. Timmins, *A history of Warwickshire,* 1889, 212-3, Langford, 12-13, FL vol 24, 241.

BEES: NQ, 12 Ser., VI, 67 and Lavery, 16-17 (ownership custom).

SUPERSTITIONS: Langford, *passim,* Timmins, 213 ff, Bennett, 92 (soapsuds), *ibid,* 50, and Coleman, 12 (Christmas).

FOLK MEDICINE: Timmins, 214, Bloom, 28-9, Langford, 15 (sneezing), *ibid,* 15 (cutting nails), Coleman, 12 (elder), FL, 1913, vol 24, 241, Powis, 30.X.43 and 6.XI.44, Bennett, 48, Bloom, 27 (whooping cough), *Gentleman's Magazine,* Oct. 1804, 909 (ash tree charm; see also *ibid,* 516), Brand vol 3, 278 (murderer's curative touch), Bennett, 88 (curative bone), NQ, 12 Ser., VII, 245-6, and Bloom, 55 (rheumatism), Powis, 30.X.1943 (roasted mouse for bed wetting), *ibid,* 6.XI.1943 (hare brains), Bloom, 28 (dowment), NQ, 12 Ser., VII, 245-6 (shingles), Bloom, 25-6 and 55 (croup and sore throat), Powis, 6.XI.1943 (tobacco smoke, infusions, chilblains), Bloom, 55, and NQ, 12 Ser., VII, 245-6 (cramp, pins and needles), *ibid, id,* and Bloom, 25-6 (white mouth and teething), *ibid,* 29-30, and NQ, 12 Ser., VII, 245-6 (scarlet fever), Bloom, 30-1, and Langford, 12 (warts), Bloom, 31 (stye), *ibid,* 55 ('If you'd live ... ').

FOOD: Northall, *Rhymes,* 300 ('belly bost'), Mr Pratt, *Harvest home,* 1805, quoted Northall, *Word-book* (under 'Groaty-pudding'), Bloom, 36 (hogs' pudding), NQ, 12 Ser., VII, 507 (apples), Bennett, 30, Powis, 4.XII.44 (bread), Langford, 24 (Ascension Day report; see also Morley, 160-1), Ashby, 67 (miller's tale), Bloom, 36-8, Bennett, 37, Powis, 4.XII.44 (beer), Bloom, 41 (Chacomb story).

6 *Foul fiend and goblin damned,* pages 71-81

DEVIL: Bloom (Meon Hill), Northall, *Phrases,* 24 (devil's nutting bag); G. Grigson, *The Englishman's flora,* 1975, 226, 228 and 67 (plants), K. Thomas, *Religion and the decline of magic,* 1973, 564 (Coventry story), Bloom, 96 (Long Compton story), Northall, *Rhymes,* 306 ('turnpike' rhyme), Bennett, 4-5 (tinder box).

SUPERNATURAL CREATURES: Timmins, 220, J. Allies, *Antiquities of Worcestershire,* 1856, 413-16, 425, 431, 438, Powis, 15.I.45 (place names), Bennett, 79, *A Midsummer Night's Dream* II i (fairy rings), *The Tempest* IV i ('played the Jack'), Allies, 438 ('mabled'), Langford, 19 (grim), Powis, 15.I.45 (cobs, etc.), Andrews, 245 (flibbertigibbet), Northall, *Phrases,* 24 (Old Flam).

GHOSTS: *Birmingham Evening Mail,* 31.10.1974, p. 16 (Civil War and female ghost at Short Heath), Coleman, 15 (phantom lorry), Bloxham, 186-9, Bett, 78, NQ, 4 Ser., V, 63, Morley, 76 (One-handed Boughton; Parson Hall is mentioned in the enclosure award for Great Harborough, 1754), F. G. Lee, *Glimpses of the supernatural,* quoted in Bloxham, 148-9 (Barby ghost), Bloom, 99, Burgess, 139 (Ilmington ghosts), FL, 1927, vol 38, 31 (Dick Turpin), Morley, 85-8 (Blacklow Hill, Guy's Cliffe and Chesford Bridge), J. Hallam, *The haunted inns of England,* 1972, 207 (Blue Lias), *ibid,* 205-6 (White Swan), Coleman, 15 (Dick's Garret, Astley Castle and Haseley Pool), *ibid,* 16, Burman, *Families,* 11, Hackwood, *Collection,* 83, Morley, 91-4 (Clopton), Bloom, 100

(Hillborough and Alscot), Burgess, 132 (Ragley), FL, 1958, vol 69, 181 (black dog at Lower Quinton), Bloom, 100 (dog at Alveston), Coleman, 15 (black dog at Whitmore Park), V. Bird, 49, quoting a Women's Institute *History scrapbook* (black dog and ectoplasm at Snitterfield), FL, 1927, vol 38, 30 (Fenny Compton ray), Bennett, 83, and Powis, 22.I.45 (Mickleton hooter), Coleman, 15 (Fillongley ghosts), source not traced (Southam), Bennett, 82 (traction engine), *Stratford Herald*, 21.7.1974, p.9 (Stratford ghost stories), Bloom, 99 (quotation).

7 *Churn, butter, churn*, pages 82-89

WITCHES: V. Bird, article in the *Sunday Mercury*, 24.3.1975 (Sarah's Oak), Langford, 18 (Ann Archer), W. C. Hazlitt, *Dictionary of faiths and folklore*, 1905, 59 (case at Stratford), E. Rainsberry, *Through the lych gate*, 1969, 126-7, Langford, 18, Bloom, 86, *Warwick Advertiser*, 25.9.1875, Morley, 65 ff (case at Long Compton), Morley, 95 (case at Brailes).

ROLLRIGHT: W. H. Hutton, 4-6, Bloom, 93, Powis, 8.I.45, FL, 1895, vol 6, 6-51, NQ 12 Ser., VII, 488 (Humphrey Boffin).

MORE WITCHES: Bloom, 97 (George Bailey story), *ibid*, 98-9 (Nance A.), Wootton, 120 (Sarah Brookes), Bloom, 95 (Mrs F.), *ibid*, 97, (Better L.), Bennett, 80, Bloom, 94 (Betty H.).

SPELLS: Bloom, 63, NQ, 12 Ser., VII, 507, Powis, 11.XI.44, Bennett, 39-40, Bloom, 96 (Mary W.), *Comedy of Errors* IV iii, Bloom, 98 (Willington story), Coleman, 10 (Billy Balson), Bloom, 96-7 (Mrs H. and Betty P.).

EVEN MORE WITCHES: Burgess, 7-9 (Moll Bloxham), Powis, 8.I.45 (sheaf of wheat), NQ,14 Ser., vol 165, 189 (Mrs Bennett of Charlecote), Tom Langley, interviewed by Roy Palmer, 1974 (obelisk).

CHARLES WALTON: this case was extensively reported in the press at the time, and has since been subject to various enquiries, including on television. One wonders whether this was the same Charles Walton who saw the supernatural dog at Alveston (see p. 79 of this book).

8 *Marriage, birth and death*, pages 90-101

MARRIAGE OMENS: Langford, 23 (cheek burning), *ibid*, 18, Savage, 364, Wise, 80 (fern seed).

WEDDINGS: Bloom, 13-15, 71, Bennett, 53, 115, Powis, 20.XI.44, 27.XI,44, 4.XII.44, F. J. Furnivall, *Captain Cox, his ballads and books. or Robert Laneham's Letter* (1575), 1871 (bride ale), G. S. Tyack, *Lore and legend of the English church,* 1899, 186 (naked bride).

MARITAL RELATIONSHIPS: Northall, *Rhymes,* 345 ('Heeper, peeper'), Timmins, 218 (Sage trees), FLJ vol 2, 1884, 187 (Chaff — from Stratford; see also *Birmingham Weekly Post,* 7.4.1888), E. Rollins (ed.), *The Pepys Ballads,* 8 vols, Harvard University Press, 1929-32: vol 3, 202 (ballad).

LEWBELLING: *Illustrated London News,* 14.8.1909, FL, 1913, vol 24, 241 (Charlecote), Bloom, 53 (Whatcote).

WIFE SELLING: Northall, *Rhymes,* 293 (Nebuchadnezzar), Bloom, 54, R. Chambers, *Book of days,* 1863-4, vol 1, 487, F. W. Hackwood, *Staffordshire customs, superstitions and folklore,* Lichfield, 1924, 70 (Hackwood gives the *Annual Register* date as 1733, but I have preferred the date of 1773 given by J. A. Langford in his *Century of Birmingham Life,* 1868, vol 1, 264. This is confirmed by an article in *The Antiquary* (vol. XVI, Jul.-Dec., 1887, p. 167) which says that the sale was recorded in a toll book kept at the Bell Inn.)

LEASE OF HUSBAND: NQ, 1 Ser., VII, 603. I am indebted for this reference to Edward Thompson.

MAN WITH THREE WIVES: Bloom, 51.

DEATH: Langford, 11, 14-16, Bennett, 71, Bloom, 42-4, Northall, *Word-book* (Winding sheet), FL, 1913, vol 24, 239-40 (parsley, mandrake), Langford, 15 (spade rhyme), Bennett, 57 (May rhyme), Powis, 4.III.45 (feathers), Bennett, 93, Langford, 15, FL, 1923, vol 34, 239 (bees), Langford, 14 (clocks), Timmins, 213 (grave left open), Purser, 16-17, Wootton, 122 (cortege), Bloom, 48-9 (corpse ways), NQ, 12 Ser., VII, 507 (pall), Cooper, 58-9, Powis, 11.III.45 (bells), Morley, 115-6 (mourning).

BIRTHS: Bennett, 53 ('Good year for nuts'), Powis. 12.XI.1944, and Bloom, 17 (evil influences), Powis, 13.XI.1944 (changelings and treacle of heaven), *ibid,* and Bloom, 26 (caul), Langford, 14 (hair on arms), *ibid,* 13-14 (Christmas Day), *ibid,* 15 (rhyme), Powis, 13.XI.1944, and Bloom, 19-20 (caudle and hare jelly), *ibid,* 26-7 (teeth), NQ, 12 Ser., VII, 245 (charms).

9 *The hobby horse forgot:* pages 102-119

TITLE: *Hamlet* III ii.

ENTERTAINMENT FOR ELIZABETH I: see Furnivall, *passim;* also *Queen Elizabeth's visit to Kenilworth, 1575,* Kenilworth, 1975.

PLAYS: Dugdale, 121 (Corpus Christi; Burbidge (p. 152) argues that Dugdale was incorrect in saying that the plays were performed by the Grey Friars; they were performed by 'the city companies and their members', and Dugdale might have been misled by informants who had seen the plays by – meaning near to – Grey Friars), Bennett, 110 (Kenilworth), FL, 1899, vol 10 (Newbold play). For other plays, see E. C. Cawte, A. Helm and N. Peacock, *English ritual drama,* 1967, 60-1.

BEAR BAITING: Furnivall, 16.

MORRIS DANCING: Furnivall, 22-3, J. H. Bird, 14-18, *Birmingham Weekly Post,* NQ, 3.5, 1884.

COTSWOLD GAMES: *Annalia Dubrensia,* 1636, *passim,* Chambers, 713, W. H. Hutton, 151-5.

VARIOUS SPORTS: V. Bird, 35, 76, Bennett, 108, Powis, 12.II.45 (kick-shins), Hackwood, *Olden,* 97 (Berkswell parson), Bennett, 110 (bumblepuppy), Purser, 14 (quoits), Wise, 156, *Merry Wives* I i (shovel board), Bloom, 142-3 (put), Savage, 327 (fox and geese).

NINE MEN'S MORRIS: Bloom, 143-4, Wise, 105, Savage, 327, *Dream* II ii, Powis, 12.II.45, Brand, Modern instructions for the game read as follows: Each player has nine men. Black starting, each player places a man in any vacant hole, in turn. When a player has three men in a straight row (except diagonally) he can remove one of his opponent's men from the board, so long as it does not form part of a line of three. When all men are placed, players move a man alternately to any vacant hole adjacent in the same line. When a player has three men, he can move to any pin vacant, whether it is adjacent in the same line or not. The game ends when either player is reduced to two men.

MORE VIGOROUS SPORTS: Ashby, 36 (wrestling), Powis, 12.II.45, Bennett, 112 (tip cat), Purser, 14 (football at Ilmington), FL, 1960, Vol 71, 195-6, (football at Atherstone).

WOODMEN OF ARDEN: Byng, vol 2, 108, Burman, *Arden,* 88-9. see also *Records of the Woodmen of Arden from 1785 to 1935,* 1937, *passim.*

BLOOD SPORTS, BEAR AND BULL BAITING: Northall, *Word-book,* 24 ('play the bear'), Northall, *Phrases*, 10 and 8 ('As rough as a bear's backside' and 'As full of megrims'), Bennett, 37 (bull beef), Hackwood, *Olden*, 28 (Bull Ring), W. Hutton, *History of Birmingham*, 1809, 206, F. W. Hackwood, *Old English sports*, 1907, 310, Dent, vol 2, 305, and vol 1, 110 (bull baiting), W. Mackay, *Ballad chronicles*, Birmingham, 1832, 28-30 (song written in 1798), Hackwood, *Olden*, 100, and Kemp, 83 (lion).

BLOOD SPORTS, COCK FIGHTING: Joseph Hill, MS Diary, 3 May and 19 Mar., 1799, *Aris's Gazette*, June 1747 (advertisement); see also 11.4.1748), *Gentleman's Magazine*, 1747, vol 17, 292 (poem), Dent, vol 2, 318 (Smallbrook advertisement), Jaffray, 52 ('It was suppressed'), *Daily News*, 26.9.1868, quoted Hazlitt, vol. 1, 138 (publican's fine), *Aris's Gazette*, 17.4.1785 (Sutton), Drew, 153-4 (Kenilworth), Morley, 226 (Leamington), Ashby, 36 ('Tysoe), V. Bird, 27 (Fell Mill Farm), Hackwood, *Old English*, 261 (Polesworth), Bennett, 108 ('No cocks' eyes'), Northall, *Phrases*, 23 ('That cock won't fight').

PRIZE FIGHTING: Burman, *Families*, 109, quoting Rev. Nash Stephenson (1843-67), Showell, 290. I am grateful to Tom Langley for allowing me to see the manuscript of his forthcoming book on Bob Brettle, which is to be published by Vance Harvey, Leicester.

SAINT MONDAY AND EIGHTEENTH CENTURY RECREATIONS: G. Davis, *Saint Monday; or, scenes from low life: a poem*, Birmingham, 1795.

MODERN ENTERTAINMENTS: see D. Read, 'The killing of Saint Monday', in *Grapevine*, Birmingham April 1975.

10 *March to wakes and fairs*, pages 120-130
TITLE: *King Lear* III vi.
SURVEY: see J. Richardson, *The local historian's encyclopedia*, 1974, 251ff.
CHARTERS: Bloom, 103.
CHERRY WAKES: Savage, 199, Bloom, 106-7, and Kemp, 83. Bloom says they were held on three Sundays in June in the orchards between Fell Mill and Shipston, and in front of the Three Stars at Stratford.
BIRMINGHAM HORSE FAIR: the plaque says that the fairs ended in 1911, but a friend of mine, Douglas French, who lived in

Birmingham in the 1920s, says they continued till then. The painting, 'The Birmingham Horse Fair', by David Cox (1783-1859), is in the City Art Gallery, Birmingham. The rhyme is in Northall, *Word-book*, 22.

FAIRS: Cooper, 2 (Henley), Drew, 125 (Crock Fair), Burman, *Arden*, 48 (Tanworth), Bennett, 70 (mop), Palmer, *Plough*, 17-18, (mop, quoting W. Hone, *Everyday book*, 1838, ed., vol III, cols 174 ff) Morley, 121-2 (song), Burman, *ibid* (Tanworth hiring), Adams, 6 (Hampton Statutes), *Sir Benjamin Stone's Pictures*, 76 (picture of Bidford and Stratford mops), Wright, vol 3, 165 (Rugby fair), Palmer, *Plough*, 18 (interview about Warwick mop), Cooper, 12 (Henley Mop), Wright, vol 3, 171-8 (Southam), G. Jaggard, *Stratford mosaic*, 1960, quoting yearly proclamation, Bennett, 109 (Stratford Mop), *Spectator*, 18.9.1711, Byng, vol. 3, 152 (grinning), Bennett, 109 (greasy pig, quoting the verse of a song), Wright, vol 3, 89 (schoolboy's account), *Kenilworth Advertiser*, 29.9.1877, quoted in J. H. Drew, *Kenilworth: an historical miscellany*, Kenilworth, 1969, 13-14 (Kenilworth Mop; see also *Kenilworth Advertiser*, 28.9.1878), J. E. Vaughan, *The parish church and ancient grammar school of King's Norton*, 1969, 8-9 (King's Norton Mop).

WAKES: A. Payne, *Portrait of a parish*, 1969, 134, NQ, 10 Ser., X, 155 (Long Itchington), Bloom, 104-5 (Newbold, Preston, Alderminster, Bearly, Snitterfield, Quinton, Tredington, Shottery, Aston Cantlow, Whatcot, Ettington, Ilmington), Cooper, 167 (Henley).

BIRMINGHAM WAKES: Deritend Wake was held on 29th August, the day on which St John was beheaded. Deritend Wake Sunday was known in Birmingham as the first day of winter. Showell, 264 (bulrushes), Dent, vol 2, 305 (Chapel Wake), W. Hutton, 205-6, and Jaffray, 53 (quotations).

BIRMINGHAM FAIRS: W. Hutton, 43-5, W. Barrow, 'Birmingham markets and fairs', in *Transactions of the Archaeological Section of the Birmingham and Midland Institute*, 1912, *passim*, Hackwood, *Olden*, ch. 7, *passim*, *Birmingham Journal*, 14.6.1851, *Birmingham Post*, 28.9.1874. I am indebted for the last two references to students at Birmingham University who staged a documentary drama on the Birmingham fairs in May 1975, under the title of *Fair Play*.

COVENTRY FAIRS: J. Lancaster, *Godiva of Coventry*, 1967, 60.

11 *Guy and Godiva*, pages 131-139

GUY: *Guardian*, 10.6.1975 (spoons), Bloxam, 170-77, *The legend of Sir Guy*, in T. Percy, *Reliques of Ancient English Poetry*, 1866-7, vol 3, 143, Puttenham, *Arte of English poesie*, 1589 Bk 2, ch. 9, quoted in J. Strutt, *The sports and pastimes of the people of England*, ed., W. Hone, 1876, 267-8 (orig. ed. 1801), C. Simpson, *The British broadside ballad and its music*, 1966, 283-5 (discussion of ballads on Sir Guy; a copy of the ballad issued in 1592, together with an illustration showing Sir Guy, is in *Roxburghe Ballads*, 1871-99, vol 6, 734-6), Dr Caius, *De rariorum animalium historia libellus*, and *The Tragical History*, *Admirable Achievements*, *and Various Events of Guy*, *Earl of Warwick*, a Tragedy, cited by Bloxam, *op. cit.*, as is Evelyn.

GODIVA: Lancaster, 44-5 (Wendover account), Percy, *op. cit.*, vol 3, 473-7 (ballad), Burbidge, 50 (Dugdale at school).

COVENTRY FAIRS: Brand, vol 1, 286 ff, Burbidge, ch. 9, *passim*, Lancaster, 55 ff, W. R. Reader, *New Coventry guide*, 1810, 112-5, quoted by Lancaster, 58-9 (1809 programme), Burbidge, 43, V. Bird, 121 (Southam), *Birmingham Post*, 21.9.1974, p. 2 (picture and article dealing with modern play).

12 *Songs of all Sizes*, pages 140-153

TITLE: *Winter's Tale* IV iv.

COX'S BALLADS: The seven listed by Laneham are: So wo iz me begon, Ouer a whinny Meg, Hey ding a ding, Bony lass vpon a green, My bony on gane me a bek, and By a bank as I lay (Furnivall, 30).

LIBEL: C. R. Baskervill, *The Elizabethan Jig*, Chicago, 1929 (reprinted New York, 1965), 66.

WARWICKSHIRE BROADSIDE BALLADS: Roy Palmer, research in progress.

BUTTON-MAKER: Madden Collection, 4/245, Cambridge University Library. The tune would appear to be the one collected by Dr George Gardiner in 1906 (published under the title of *Gaol Song* in F. Purslow, *The foggy dew*, 1974, 32). The second printed version mentioned is in undated garland entitled *The Birmingham Button-Maker* in Harvard University Library (see W. C. Lane (ed.), *Catalogue of English and American chapbooks and broadside ballads in Harvard College Library*, Cambridge, Mass., 1905).

BALLAD SELLERS: W. Marshall, *Rural economy of the Midland Counties*, 1790, vol 2, 20-1 (Polesworth), J. A. Langford, *Century*, 1868, vol 2, 44 (Birmingham notice, dated 20 May 1794), Madden Collection, 21/428 (Russell's list).

YOUNG HENRY: Madden, 21/565, printed by Jackson and Son (late J. Russell), Birmingham.

WOOD'S BALLADS: see *Scrapbook* in Birmingham Reference Library (no. 50987).

MOON SHINES BRIGHT: M. Karpeles (ed.), *Cecil Sharp's Collection of English Folk Songs*, 1974, no. 367A and note, p. 633.

DIVES AND LAZARUS: Miller, 41-2.

WIMPSTONE CAROLS: Bloom, 114.

THE CARNAL AND THE CRANE: W. Hone, *Ancient mysteries*, 1823, 93.

TYSOE: Ashby, 68.

THE CRUEL GARDENER AND LORD THOMAS: Bloom, 132-3.

I WISH, I WISH: Northall, *Word-book*, 277-8.

THE BITTER WITHY: Savage, 182-3. See also FL, 1908, vol 19, 192.

THE HOLLY AND THE IVY: Savage, 159-60.

THE KEEPER: Karpeles, no. 271A; collected by Sharp in 1909.

BALLAD-SINGERS: Drew, *Miscellany*, 37-8, quoting the *Warwick Advertiser*, 20.2.1847 (Luke Sturley, who died in 1843 'in the 89th year of his age', having been parish clerk for 'upwards of 60 years'. His epitaph reads: The graves around for many a year/ Were dug by him who slumbers here/Till worn with age he dropped his spade/And in this dust his bones were laid/As he now mouldering shares the doom/Of those he buried in the tomb/So will his body too with theirs arise/To share the judgement of the skies), Savage, 350 (Shipston singer; could this be John Bradley, from whom Sharp collected a number of songs? – see Karpeles nos. 183C, 278C, 306 and 315A), W. Tomlinson, 'A bunch of street ballads', *Papers of the Manchester Literary Club*, vol. 12, 1866, 308, *Birmingham Daily Gazette*, 25.9.1865 (I am indebted for this reference to Mr Doug Read), *Birmingham Weekly Mercury*, 20.11.1886.

AYE FOR SATURDAY NIGHT: Palmer, *Songs*, 33. On record, sung by

Joan Smith (*The wide Midlands,* Topic Record 12TS210, 1971). Mrs Costello herself can be heard singing on Leader Record LEE4054, 1975.

BRUMMAGEM MARY: sung by Mr E. W. Simmons of Stirchley, Birmingham; collected by Roy Palmer, 12th Dec. 1971 (unpublished). Kynoch's: arms factory; Pairsher Road: Pershore Road.

SUMMER LANE: sung by Mr Laurence 'Pummy' Rogers of Sheldon, Birmingham; collected by Roy Palmer, 20 July 1975. Mr Rogers learned the song from a friend who claimed to have learned it from the man who wrote it. Several versions of the song are still circulating in Birmingham, among people who formerly lived in the Summer Lane area. Mrs Mary Evans of Erdington has a variant on the chorus (collected by Roy Palmer, 11th Oct. 1971; unpublished), and Mr Bill Downing of Edgbaston has a version differing slightly from Mr Rogers', including the line, 'Then down Steelhouse Lane a tram you'll catch' (*Birmingham Evening Mail,* 16.7.1975, p. 5). Cutlers was a well-known pub on the corner of Station Street and Hurst Street. The Black Patch, according to Mr Rogers, was either the old Serpentine Grounds at Aston, or an area in Ladywood.

THEY'RE CHANGING: written by Mr G. S. Miles of Birmingham, 1972.

THE FIRST TIME: sung by Hazel Dagless, Tina Haynes, Jacqueline Bluck, Sandra Evans, Beverley Barker, Helena Romanowski, and Jennifer Cox (all aged 13) of Birmingham; collected by Roy Palmer, Feb. 1966. There is ample evidence that this tradition continues: see, for example, the article on playground song in Birmingham, 'Rhyme, rhythm and song,' by Pat Palmer (*The Times Educational Supplement,* 3.10.1975, p.26).

13 *The everlasting circle,* pages 154-172
JANUARY
NEW YEAR: Langford, 21, Mrs Elsie Marshall, interviewed by Katharine Thomson, 1966. For the tune of her song, see Palmer, *Songs,* 11; cf Northall, *Rhymes,* 182-3, and Morley, 146.
GOD CAKES: NQ, 2 Ser., II, 229, Wright, vol 2, 29, Burbidge, 42.
PLOUGH MONDAY: Bloom, 80.
FEBRUARY
Bloom, 115 (Candlemas), Ashby, 20, and Bloom, 115 (Valentine),

Birmingham Post, 12.2.1975 (pancake race at Alcester), Joseph Hill, MS diary, 5th Feb. 1799 (throwing at cocks at Stratford), Burbidge, 192 and 73 (throwing at cocks at Coventry).

MARCH

MOTHERING SUNDAY: Bloom, 116, Morley, 104, Northall, *Word-book*, 86 (frumenty).

APRIL

Bloxam, 159 (Fools at Rugby), Brand, vol 1, 12 (hares at Coleshill), Palmer, *Touch*, 78 (song, under the title of *I can't find Brummagem*; it was written in 1828), W. Hone, *The Every-day Book*, 1838, vol. 1, 431 (church clipping), Morley, 106-7, Brand, vol 1, 183-4, Hone, vol 1, 425, Showell, 264, Miller, 51 (heaving), Burbidge, 67 (bonfires), *ibid*, 69 (Hock Tuesday), *ibid*, 43 (St George).

MAY

Dream I i, Burbidge, 72 (at Coventry), W. H. Hutton, 275-6 (at Henley), Vaughan, 9, 27-8 (at King's Norton), W. Gardiner, *Music and friends*, 1838-53, vol 1, 444, 446, 450, Hone, vol 2, 575-7 (Dr Parr), Kemp, 88-9 (Warwick), FLJ 1883, vol 1, 353 (Sarah Chandler's account), Bloom, 121-2, Morley, 109-110, (Children), Bloom, 122, Burbidge, 72-3 (sweeps), Northall, *Word-book*, 161, Showell, 193, Powis 26 II 45, Wright, vol 2, 263, 265 (Oak Apple Day), Morley, 111-112 (seagulls), Bloom, 64, FLJ, 1883, vol 1, 352-3 (Whitsun).

JUNE

Bird, 159 (Wroxall), C. Wharton, 'Warwickshire calendar customs', in *Warwickshire history*, vol 1, no. 5, Spring 1971, 7 (Ascension Day at St Mary's, Warwick), Savage, 140, 170-1, Morley, 113, Drew, 45 ff, Bloom, 121 (beating bounds), Bloom, 125 (Barnabas), Burbidge, 67-8 (midsummer bonfires), Wise, 80 (fern seed).

JULY

Ashby, 68-9 (Club Week at Tysoe).

AUGUST

Gutteridge, 83, Wright, vol 3, 44 (Lammas riding).

SEPTEMBER

Morley, 12 (removing).

OCTOBER

J. Salisbury, *A glossary of words and phrases used in S. E.*

Worcestershire, 1893, 65-6, quoting *Evesham Standard*, 7.10.1893 (candle auction), NQ, 9 Ser., VI, 449 (price control), private communication 20.2.1975 from the Headmaster, Mr P. W. Martin (Warwick School), Kemp, 87 (beating bounds), Wootton, 107 (Hallowe'en at Knowle).

NOVEMBER

Two Gentlemen II ii, FL, 1914, vol 25, 293 (souling), Bloom, 127 (bonfire night), Bird, 170-1 (Wroth Money – oddly enough, this ceremony is not mentioned in the first edition of Dugdale, 1656, though it comes into Dr Thomas' second edition of 1730. Stone has some pictures. See also *The Antiquary*, vol. XII, Jul.-Sept., 1885, 110), Langford, 21, FL, 1914, vol 25, 293, *The Times*, 10.12.1925, p. 17, col. d (referring to '50 years ago'), Wright, vol 3, 176, Northall, *Rhymes*, 222 (Clement's), Showell, 18 (barring out)

DECEMBER

Wright, vol 3, 208 (Duchess Dudley), Brand, vol 1, 456, Morley, 133, 139 (St Thomas), Wright, vol 2, 74, Morley, 144 (animals on Christmas Eve), Morley, 145 (bees), *Gentleman's Magazine*, 1795, 110 (Aston Hall ceremony), FL, 1883, vol 1, 351-2, (Sarah Chandler's account), Morley, 142 (log rhyme), FLJ, 1883, vol 1, 352, Wright, vol 3, 242, Savage, 195 (wassail from 'a jovial villager').

Select Bibliography

J. C. ADAMS, *Hampton-in-Arden*, Birmingham, n.d.

W. ANDREWS, *Bygone Warwickshire*, Hull, 1893

M. K. ASHBY, *Joseph Ashby of Tysoe, 1859-1919*, Cambridge, 1961

W. BARROW, 'Birmingham markets and fairs', in *Transactions of the Archaeological Section of the Birmingham and Midland Institute*, Birmingham, 1912

F. W. BENNETT, *Tiddyoody pie*, no imprint, 1930

H. BETT, *English myths and traditions*, London, 1952

J. H. BIRD, *Sam Bennett, the Ilmington fiddler*, Stratford-on-Avon, 1952

V. BIRD, *Warwickshire*, London, 1973

J. H. BLOOM, *Folk lore, old customs and superstitions in Shakespeare land*, London, 1930

M. H. BLOXHAM, *Rugby, the school and neighbourhood: history and legends of Rugby and neighbourhood*, London, 1889

J. BRAND, *Observations on the popular antiquities of Great Britain*, 3 vols, London, 1849

K. M. BRIGGS, *A dictionary of British folk tales*, 4 vols, London, 1970-1.

F. B. BURBIDGE, *Old Coventry and Lady Godiva*, Birmingham, 1952

A. BURGESS, *Warwickshire*, London, 1950

J. BURMAN, *Old Warwickshire families and their houses*, Birmingham, 1934; *In the forest of Arden*, Birmingham, 1948

J. BYNG, *The Torrington diaries*, 4 vols, London, 1934-8

R. CHAMBERS, *The Book of Days*, 2 vols, London, 1863

S. J. COLEMAN, *Warwickshire folklore*, Douglas, I.O.M., 1952

W. COOPER, *Henley-in-Arden*, Birmingham, 1946

R. CROMPTON-RHODES, *A Birmingham glossary* (unpublished typescript in Birmingham Reference Library, no. 662306)

R. K. DENT, *Old and new Birmingham*, 2 vols, 1878-80; reprinted in 3 vols, Wakefield, 1972-3

J. H. DREW, *Kenilworth, a manor of the king*, Kenilworth, 1971

W. DUGDALE, *The antiquities of Warwickshire*, London 1656; 2nd ed., 1730; another ed., Coventry, 1765

H. N. ELLACOMBE, *The plant-lore and garden-craft of Shakespeare*, Exeter, 1878

F. J. FURNIVALL, *Captain Cox, his ballads and books; or Robert Laneham's letter* (1575), London, 1871

C. F. GREEN, *The legend of Shakespeare's Crab-tree*, London, 1857

J. GUTTERIDGE, *Lights and shadows in the life of an artisan*, London, 1893; reprinted in V. E. Chancellor (ed.), *Master and artisan in Victorian England*, London, 1969

F. W. HACKWOOD, *A collection of newspaper cuttings relating to Warwickshire*, 1903-16, Birmingham Reference Library; *Warwickshire lore*, newspaper cuttings from the *Birmingham Weekly Mercury*, 1918-25, Birmingham Reference Library; *Olden Warwickshire: its history, lore and legend*, Birmingham, 1921

J. HALLAM, *The haunted inns of England*, London, 1972

C. G. HARPER, *Summer days in Shakespeare land*, London, 1912

W. C. HAZLITT, *Dictionary of faiths and folklore*, London, 2 vols, 1905

J. HILL, *Diary*, (manuscript in private collection, xerox copy in the author's possession)

W. HONE, *The Every-day book and table book*, 3 vols, London, 1838

W. HUTTON, *An history of Birmingham*, Birmingham, 4th ed., 1809

W. H. HUTTON, *Highways and byways in Shakespeare's country*, London, 1914

J. JAFFRAY, *Hints for a history of Birmingham*, cuttings from the *Birmingham Journal*, 1855-6 (Birmingham Reference Library)

T. KEMP, *A history of Warwick and its people*, Warwick, 1905

J. C. LANCASTER, *Godiva of Coventry*, Coventry, 1967

J. A. LANGFORD, 'Warwickshire folklore and superstitions', in *Transactions of the Archaeological Section of the Birmingham and Midland Institute*, Birmingham, 1878 (written in 1875)

P. LAVERY, *Warwickshire in 1790*, Reading, 1974

A. MEE, *Warwickshire*, London, 1966

G. MILLER, *Rambles round the Edge Hills and in the Vale of the Red Horse*, Kineton, 1967 (reprint of 2nd ed. of 1900)

G. MORLEY, *Shakespeare's greenwood: the customs of the county*, London, 1900

G. F. NORTHALL, *English Folk-Rhymes*, London, 1892; *Folk phrases of four counties*, London, 1894; *A Warwickshire word-book*, London, 1896

Notes and Queries, 1849- (in progress)

R. PALMER, *The painful plough*, Cambridge, 1972; *Songs of the Midlands*, Wakefield, 1972; *A touch on the times*, Harmondsworth, 1974

A. PAYNE, *Portrait of a parish*, Kineton, 1968

M[ARJORIE] H. P[OWIS], *Warwickshire's wealth of fancies*, cuttings from the *Birmingham News*, 1943-5, (Birmingham Reference Library)

J. PURSER, *Our Ilmington*, 1966 (typescript lodged in Warwickshire County Library)

E. RAINSBERRY, *Through the lych gate*, Kineton, 1969

F. SAVAGE, *The flora and folk-lore of Shakespeare*, Cheltenham, 1923

Sir Benjamin Stone's Pictures, 2 vols in one, London, n.d.

T. F. THISTLETON DYER, *Folk lore of Shakespeare*, London, 1883

S. TIMMINS, *A history of Warwickshire*, London, 1889

J. E. VAUGHAN, *The parish church and ancient grammar school of King's Norton*, Gloucester, 1969

C. WHARTON, 'Warwickshire calendar customs', in *Warwickshire History*, vol 1, no 5, Warwick, Spring 1971

J. R. WISE, *Shakespeare: his birthplace and its neighbourhood*, London, 1861

E. WOOTTON, *The history of Knowle*, Kineton, 1972

A. R. WRIGHT and T. E. LONES, *British calendar customs: England*, 3 vols, London, 1938-40

Folk Museums

Museums of Warwickshire life are to be found at St John's House, Warwick, Grey Friars, Coventry, Blakesley Hall, Birmingham, Wilmcote (Mary Arden's House) and Shottery (Anne Hathaway's Cottage).

Index of Tale Types

Folktales are named and classified on an international system based on their plots, devised by Antti Aarne and Stith Thompson in *The Types of the Folktale*, 1961; numbers from this system are preceded by the letters AT. Local legends were partly classified by R. Th. Christiansen in *The Migratory Legends*, 1958; his system was further developed by K. M. Briggs in *A Dictionary of British Folktales*, 1970-1. These numbers are preceded by ML, and the latter are also given an asterisk.

Motif Index

A motif is an element occurring within the plot of one or several folktales (e.g. 'cruel stepmother', found in 'Snow White', 'Cinderella', etc). These have been classified thematically in Stith Thompson's *Motif Index of Folk Literature*, 1966; the numbers below are taken from this and from E. Baughman's *Type and Motif Index of the Folktales of England and North America*, 1966.

General Index